THE COINAGE OF THE EARLY OR IMPERIAL GUPTA DYNASTY OF NORTHERN INDIA

THE COINAGE OF THE EARLY OR IMPERIAL GUPTA DYNASTY OF NORTHERN INDIA

VINCENT ARTHUR SMITH

GYAN

Published by

GYAN

Gyan Publishing House
5, Ansari Road
Daryaganj, New Delhi-110002
Phone: 011-47034999, 9811692060
E-mail: books@gyanbooks.com

Distribution Network
gyanbooks.com
India, USA, Canada, UK, Australia

ISBN: 978-93-7133-071-8 (PB)

First Published, 1889

2nd Impression 2025

Printed at: Gyan Press, Delhi.

THE COINAGE OF THE EARLY OR IMPERIAL GUPTA DYNASTY OF NORTHERN INDIA

Author: VINCENT ARTHUR SMITH

The Coinage Of The Early Or Imperial Gupta Dynasty Of Northern India

Vincent Arthur Smith

1889

PLATE I

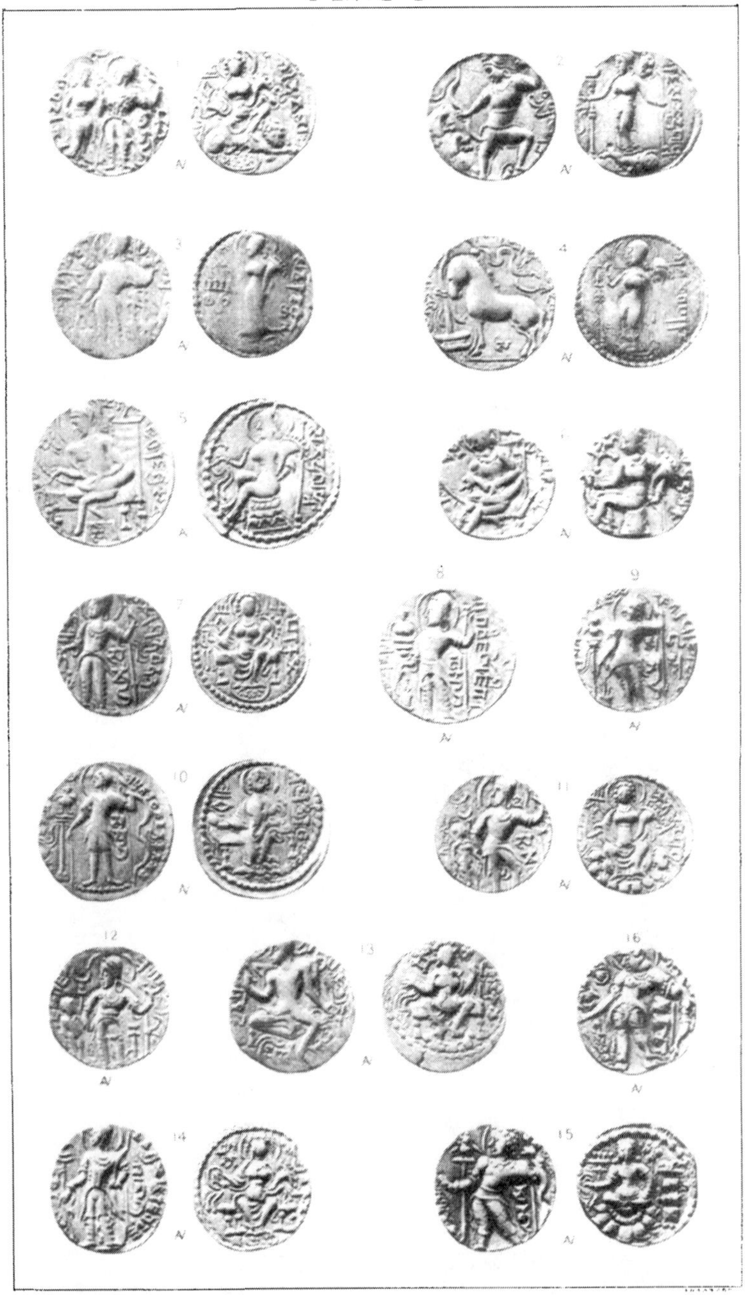

GUPTA GOLD COINS.

Plate II.

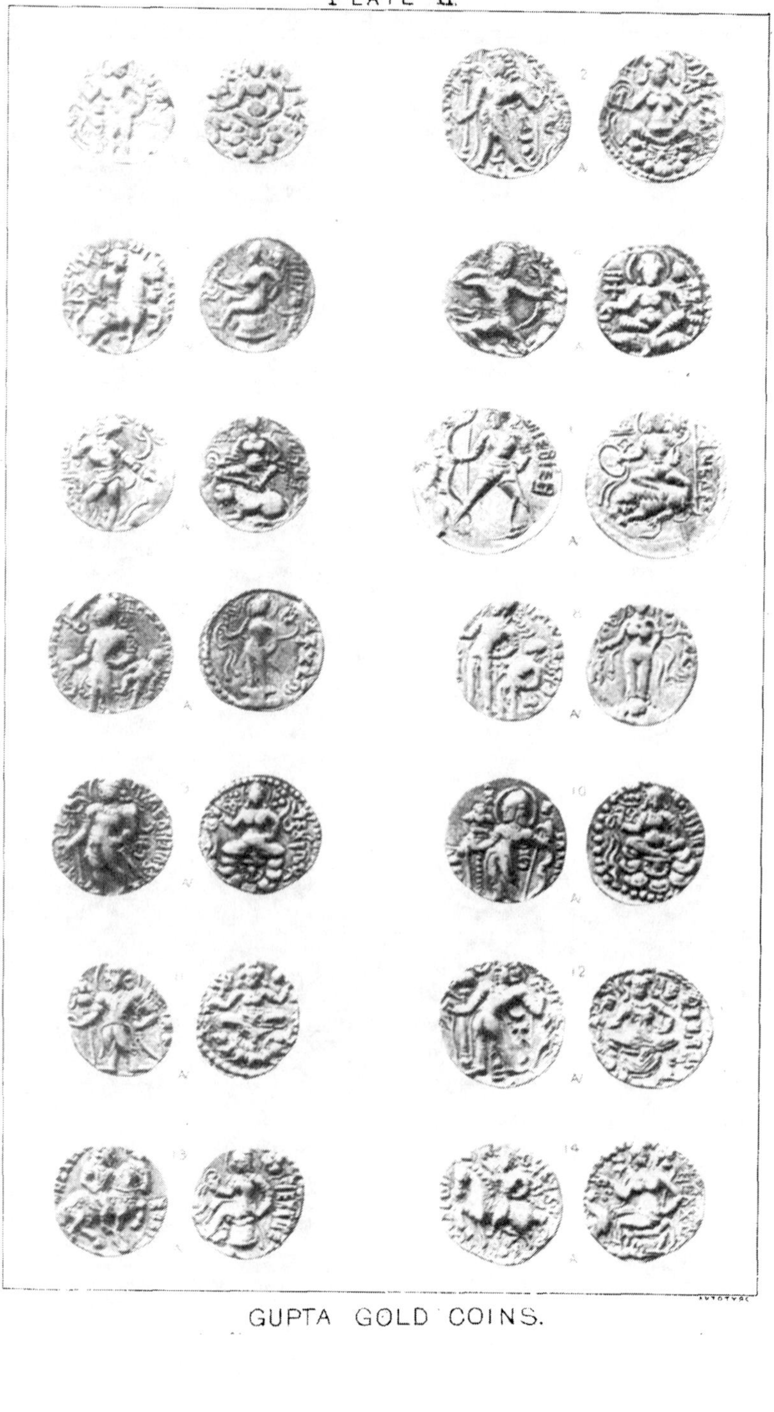

GUPTA GOLD COINS.

PLATE III.

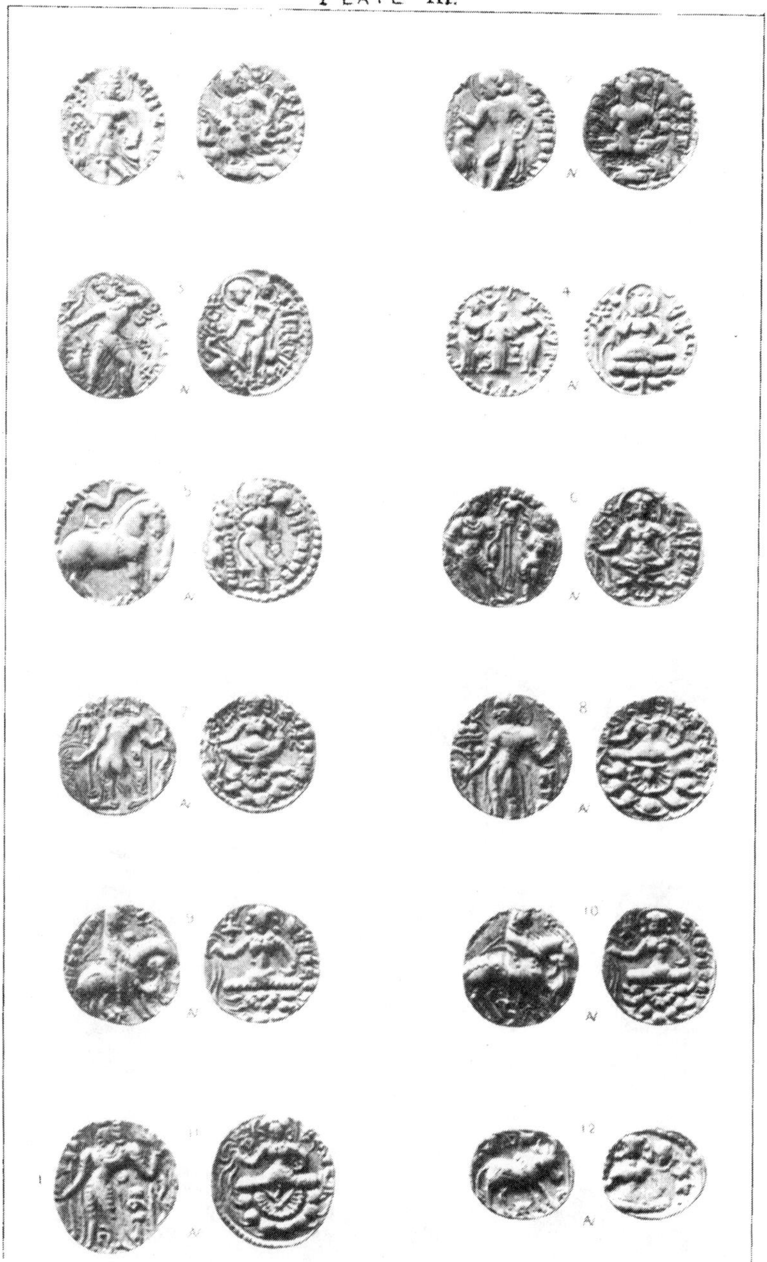

GUPTA GOLD COINS.

PLATE IV.

GUPTA SILVER AND COPPER COINS.

Plate V

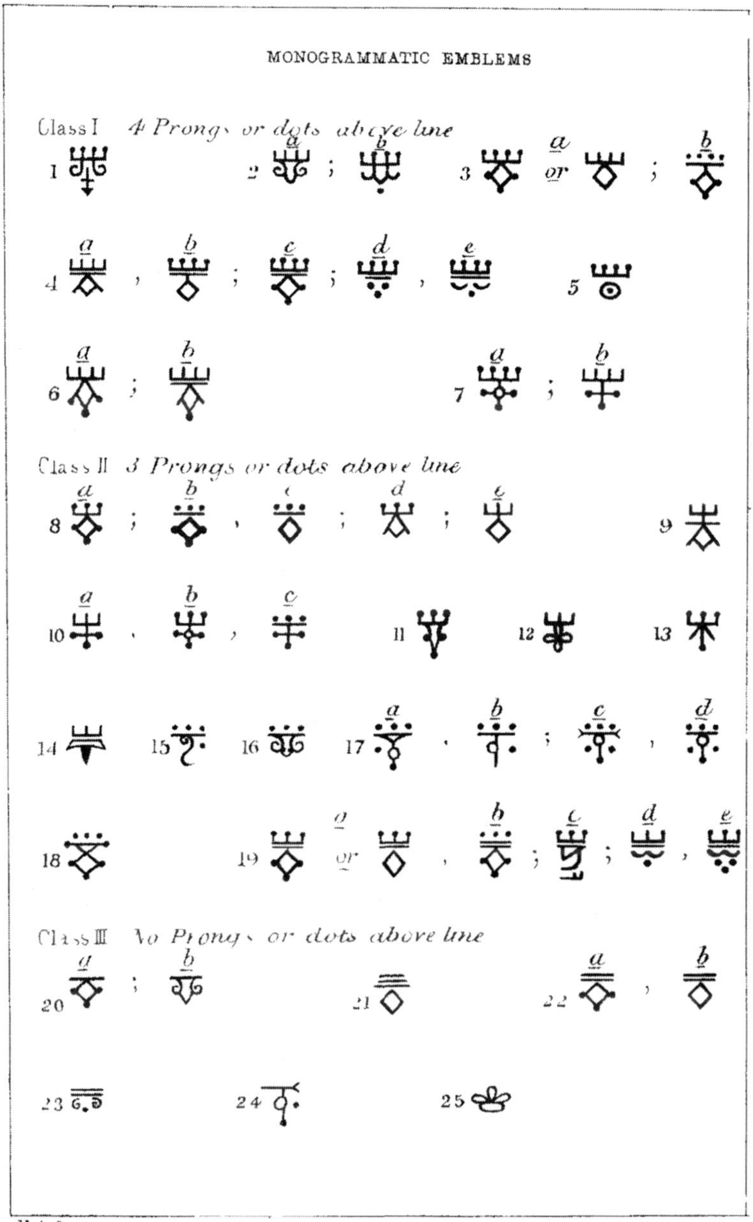

V A Smith del

W Griggs Photo-lith. Peckham S E

MONOGRAMMATIC EMBLEMS ON GUPTA GOLD COINS.

JOURNAL

OF

THE ROYAL ASIATIC SOCIETY.

ART. I.—*The Coinage of the Early or Imperial Gupta Dynasty of Northern India.* By VINCENT ARTHUR SMITH, M.R.A.S., Bengal Civil Service. With five Plates.

CONTENTS.

ABBREVIATIONS.

A.A. H. H. Wilson's Ariana Antiqua.

A.C. Cabinet of Major-General Sir Alexander Cunningham, K.C.I.E., etc.

Æ. Copper.

A.G.	Cabinet of Alexander Grant, C.I.E.[1]
AR.	Silver.
Arch.Rep.	Reports of the Archæological Survey of India, volumes i.-xxiii., written or edited by Sir A. Cunningham.
A.S.B.	Cabinet of Asiatic Society of Bengal.
AV.	Gold.
B.	Cabinet of Bodleian Library, Oxford.
B.M.	British Museum.
Boys.	Cabinet of H. S. Boys, B.C.S.
C.	Cabinet of H. Rivett-Carnac, C.I.E., B.C.S.
Diam.	Diameter in decimals of an inch.
E.C.B.	Cabinet of the late Sir E. C. Bayley, K.C.S.I.
H.	Cabinet of J. Hooper, B.C.S.
Ind.Ant.	Indian Antiquary (Bombay).
I.O.	Cabinet of India Office (now in B.M.).
J.A.S.B.	Journal of the Asiatic Society of Bengal.
J.Bo.Br.R.A.S.	Journal of the Bombay Branch of the Royal Asiatic Society of Great Britain and Ireland.
J.R.A.S.	Journal of the Royal Asiatic Society of Great Britain and Ireland.
l.	Left of reader, when used to denote position on coin; proper left, when used to denote parts of the body.
M.	Marsden's Numismata Orientalia.
Mon.	Monogram, or monogrammatic emblem.
Obv.	Obverse.
P.E.	Prinsep's Essays on Indian Antiquities, ed. Thomas (London, 1858).
Proc.A.S.B.	Proceedings of the Asiatic Society of Bengal.
r.	Right of reader, when used to denote position on coin; proper right, when used to denote parts of the body.
Records.	Records of the Gupta Dynasty, by E. Thomas (London, Trübner & Co., 1876).
Rev.	Reverse.
S.	Cabinet of J. Sykes, Barrister-at-Law, Lucknow.
Wt.	Weight in English grains.
W.T.	Cabinet of W. Theobald.

[1] Mr. A. Grant's gold Gupta coins are now in the Ermitage Impérial at St. Petersburg.

Prefatory Note.

My paper entitled 'A Classified and Detailed Catalogue of the Gold Coins of the Imperial Gupta Dynasty of Northern India, with an Introductory Essay,' written in 1883, and published in 1884 by the Asiatic Society of Bengal, gave a full account of the Gupta gold coinage, so far as it was then known. At that time it was not in my power to extend my investigations to the silver and copper coinage, and subsequent criticism and study showed that my discussion of the gold coins was in some respects defective and erroneous. An interval of rest from official work has now given me an opportunity of resuming my numismatic studies, and of completing and bringing up to date my examination of the Gupta coinage.

Numismatic science is fortunately progressive, and in course of time fresh discoveries and researches necessarily superannuate every treatise. In the following pages I have endeavoured to include all information concerning the Gupta coinage in gold, silver, and copper, which is at present available, but I cannot profess to have exhausted my subject, limited though it is, and have no doubt that the publication of this monograph will, like that of its predecessor, elicit new facts, and necessitate correction in some of the views now expressed.

I have re-examined all the gold Gupta coins in the British Museum, and have studied the fine Bodleian collection, respecting which the information previously supplied to me was very defective. The additional knowledge thus obtained, and much other detailed information derived from various sources, have enabled me to make many additions to, and corrections in, the account of the gold coinage, which has been re-written throughout.

The copper coinage is now discussed in detail for the first time. It is, of course, much less interesting than the gold coinage, so remarkable for variety of type, but appears to me not unworthy of attention.

The silver coins have been described at considerable length

by previous writers, and I have not very much that is new to say about them, but I hope that the orderly arrangement of all available information on the subject will be welcome and useful.

My obligations to the gentlemen who helped me in preparing the catalogue of the gold coins are on record, and my acknowledgments to them need not now be repeated. On the present occasion I have much pleasure in tendering my special thanks for assistance rendered by Major-General Sir A. Cunningham, K.C.I.E.; Mr. J. F. Fleet, C.I E.; Dr. A. F. Rudolf Hoernlé; Mr. E. Nicholson, Bodley Librarian; Messrs. Grueber and Rapson of the Coin Room in the British Museum; and Mr. W. Theobald. Sir A. Cunningham, with his usual liberality, placed his unrivalled cabinet and knowledge at my disposal, and, so far as I could venture to trespass on his kindness, I have made use of both. Mr. Fleet favoured me with proofs of his great work on the Gupta inscriptions, which determines the date of the coins discussed in the following pages, and the remaining gentlemen named have given me much valuable help in various ways. My minor obligations to other gentlemen are duly acknowledged in the text or footnotes.

The favourable reception accorded to my previous imperfect essay encourages me to hope that its more complete successor may prove of interest to the limited class of readers whom it concerns, and that it may stimulate further research in that section of the Indian numismatic field, which seems to me to offer a harvest more varied and abundant than that produced by any other. Coins interest me only as being documents illustrative of history—artistic, linguistic, social, religious, and political—and, when closely interrogated, they can be forced to answer questions in every department of history. The minute description and discussion of uncurrent pieces of old metal appears to many to be no better than elaborate trifling, and is best justified by the aphorism of Saint-Hilaire: "La Numismatique est patiente, et elle amasse les faits spéciaux qui la concernent, jusqu'à ce que l'histoire vienne plus tard en donner la véritable clef, si jamais elle le peut." In India history often fails to answer the call of her numismatic sister, but the study of the Gupta coinage derives a special interest from the fact that it rests throughout on independent historical documents, which it amplifies and illustrates.

Chapter I.—Historical Introduction.

The Indo-Scythian dynasties which governed Northern India during the first three centuries of the Christian era were displaced in the fourth century throughout their dominions, except the Panjâb, where they continued to rule, by a dynasty known by the name of its progenitor Gupta,[1] whose personal appellation was adopted as a family name by all his successors, save one.

This dynasty is called by Mr. Fleet that of the Early Guptas, in order to distinguish it from other reigning houses with the same family name which held sway in Magadha and elsewhere in times subsequent to its fall.

In my previous publication on the subject I called it the Imperial Gupta dynasty in order to emphasize the fact that it is distinguished from its provincial successors by the imperial rule which it exercised over all Northern India, from Nepâl to the Narbadâ River, and from Western Bengal to the Gulf of Kachchh. The term Imperial still seems to me preferable to the purely relative term Early.

When I formerly described the Gupta gold coins, the difficult problem of the Gupta chronology was still unsolved, and I followed high authority in provisionally accepting an erroneous solution. Mr. J. F. Fleet's recent researches have demonstrated that the kings of the Early or Imperial Gupta Dynasty dated their inscriptions and coins in an era, com-

[1] I formerly followed other writers in calling this prince by the name of S'rî Gupta, that is to say, in treating the honorific prefix S'rî as an integral part of the name. But I now admit the validity of the arguments adduced by Mr. Fleet to show that his name was simply Gupta (*Ind. Ant.* vol. xiv. p. 94; *Corpus Inscr. Ind.* vol. iii. p. 8, note 3). I take this opportunity of correcting the mistake I made in supposing that Sir A. Cunningham agreed with Mr. Thomas in erroneously assigning a certain silver coin to (S'rî) Gupta. Sir A. Cunningham assures me that he never did so. I misinterpreted a passage in one of his letters.

monly called the Gupta Era, of which the year A.D. 320-21 was the year 1. This fact has been proved beyond all reasonable doubt, and the proof of it has reduced the history of Northern India during the early centuries of the Christian era from chaos to order.[1]

The numerous inscriptions of the Imperial Guptas, confirmed by the numismatic evidence, prove that their dynasty consisted of seven princes, lineally connected as father and son; namely,

(1)	*Mahârâjâ*	Gupta	Acc. *circa* A.D. 300.
(2)	,,	Ghaṭotkacha [2]	,, ,, ,, 315.
(3)	*Mahârâjâdhirâjâ*	Chandra Gupta I.	Acc. *circa* A.D. 340. Married Kumâra Devî of the Lichchhavi or Lichchhivi family of Nepâl.[3]
(4)	,,	Samudra Gupta.	Acc. *circa* A.D. 365. Married Dattadevî. Probably identical with Kâcha.
(5)	,,	Chandra Gupta II.	Acc. *circa* A.D. 390. Married Dhruvadevî.
(6)	,,	Kumâra Gupta.	Acc. *circa* A.D. 414.
(7)	,,	Skanda Gupta.	,, ,, ,, 452. Died *circa* A.D. 480.

The first two princes, who bore only the inferior title of Mahârâjâ, were evidently local chiefs, and probably ruled

[1] The detailed proof will be found in the Introduction to volume iii. of the Corpus Inscriptionum Indicarum, and in a less complete form in Ind. Ant. vol. xv. p. 279, etc.

[2] The name Ghaṭotkacha is in form a compound of *ghaṭa* and *utkacha*, with the nonsensical meaning of 'a jar with hair on end.' It is probably a foreign name Sanskritised. The name is of rare occurrence, but is given in the Mahâbhârata to the son of Bhîma by Hiḍimbâ (*Ind. Ant.* vol. xiv. June, 1885), and also designates a small group of caves near Ajanṭâ, dating from A.D. 500 or 600. (*Fergusson and Burgess, Cave Temples of India*, pp. 186, 346; *Arch. Survey W.I.* vol. iv. p. 60). The name of the king Ghaṭotkacha does not occur in the Tuśâm inscription, as was formerly supposed (*Corpus Inscr. Ind.* vol. iii. p. 269, No. 67).

[3] Recent research has shown that two contemporary dynasties ruled in Nepâl. The Lichchhavi or Sûryavanśî family had its capital at Mânagṛiha, and seems to have ruled Eastern Nepâl. The rival Ṭhakurî family had its capital at Kailâsâkûṭabhavana, and apparently governed Western Nepâl. The Lichchhavi family used the era which was adopted by the Guptas, perhaps in the reign of Chandra Gupta I, while the Ṭhakurî dynasty employed the era of Harsha Vardhana (A.D. 606). Our earliest Nepâl inscriptions belong to the seventh century A.D. (*Ind. Ant.* vol. xiv. p. 349, and *Corpus Inscr. Ind.* vol. iii. *Introduction*).

in Magadha or Bihâr, subject to the suzerainty of an Indo-Scythian over-lord.

The third prince, Chandra Gupta I., who married into the Lichchhavi family, then ruling in Nepâl, assumed the higher title of Mahârâjâdhirâja, or sovereign of Mahârâjâs, and appears to have been the real founder of the greatness of his house. But we have no specific knowledge of the events of his reign, nor of those of the reigns of his predecessors.

Samudra Gupta, son and successor of Chandra Gupta I., was undoubtedly a very powerful sovereign, whose authority extended over the greater part of Northern India. The extent of his dominions is described with considerable detail in the celebrated inscription on the pillar of Aśoka in the Fort at Allâhâbâd, which was recorded early in the reign of his successor.

This successor bore, according to Hindu custom, the same name as his grandfather, and is known to us as Chandra Gupta II. With him begins the series of contemporary epigraphical records.[1] Inscriptions of his reign are dated in 82, 88, and 93 G.E., equivalent to the years A.D. 401-2, 407-8, and 412-13, and we cannot be far wrong if we assume that his reign began in or about the year A.D. 390. By making the usual allowance of twenty-five years for each generation, we obtain the dates 365 and 340 A.D. respectively for the accession of Samudra Gupta and Chandra Gupta I., as above stated.

The limiting dates of the reign of Kumâra Gupta are known with certainty, subject to a possible error of a year or two. Kumâra Gupta enjoyed a very long reign, which began in or about the year A.D. 414, and lasted probably till A.D. 452, when Skanda Gupta ascended the throne, of which

[1] The Gayâ copper-plate inscription, dated in the year 9, purports to have been executed at Ayodhyâ by order of Samudra Gupta; but Mr. Fleet shows that the document is an ancient forgery, probably executed about the beginning of the eighth century A.D. The seal, however, "is in all probability a genuine one of Samudra Gupta, detached from another plate." But it is too much worn to be of value as a contemporary record (*Corpus Inscr. Ind.* vol. iii. p. 254, No. 60). The era in which the grant purports to be dated is not specified, but if the forger meant to use the so-called Gupta era, he must have believed that Samudra Gupta was reigning in A.D. 328-29, and it is hardly possible that the belief was correct. The forger may have meant the regnal year.

he retained possession, certainly, till A.D. 467, and, probably, till A.D. 480.

We know that the dominions of Skanda Gupta extended from the borders of Eastern Nepâl to the shores of the Gulf of Kachchh, and that his peace was disturbed by the inroads of a tribe of foreigners named Hûṇas. Their attacks ultimately broke up the great Gupta empire, and Skanda Gupta was the last of his house who enjoyed imperial dignity and power. In a portion of his western dominions he was succeeded by Budha Gupta, very probably his son, whose inscription dated 165 G.E.,=A.D. 484-85, is at Eraṇ in the Sâgar District of the Central Provinces. Coins prove that Budha Gupta was still ruling his diminished territory in A.D. 500, or a year or two later.

Budha Gupta appears to have been succeeded in the west by the Hûṇa chiefs Toramâṇa and Mihirakula, who have left both inscriptions and coins as memorials of their reigns.

In Eastern Magadha, at the eastern extremity of his dominions, Skanda Gupta was immediately succeeded (*circa* A.D. 480) by Krishṇa Gupta, who was doubtless a son or other near relative of the deceased Emperor. Krishṇa Gupta was followed by ten princes of his line, the last of whom was Jîvita Gupta II., who came to the provincial throne about A.D. 720. This dynasty is known as that of the Later Guptas of Magadha, and appears to have possessed only a very local authority. During the period of its rule Western Magadha was governed by the rival, and often hostile, dynasty of the Maukharî, or Mukhara, kings, whose names generally ended with the word Varman or Varmâ. During the reign of the great king Harsha Vardhana of Kanauj (A.D. 606-7 to A.D. 648) all Northern India, including Magadha with its local chiefs, was subject to his suzerainty.[1]

Besides the Later Guptas of Eastern Magadha we find traces of other minor Gupta dynasties in Orissa and elsewhere, all perhaps connected with that imperial race which had

[1] The foregoing historical summary is based on Mr. Fleet's work on the Gupta Inscriptions, vol. iii. of the Corpus Inscr. Ind.

exercised sovereign power for about a century and a half.[1]

I propose to confine my detailed discussion and description of the Gupta coinage to that of the Imperial Dynasty and of Budha Gupta. An exhaustive examination of the coinages of Toramâṇa, Mihirakula, the Later Guptas of Magadha, the Nâgas of Narwâr, and the other mintages more or less closely connected with the coinage of the Imperial Guptas, would, even if I were prepared to undertake it, expand my work beyond all reasonable limits, and I have preferred to confine myself to a compact, well-defined subject, which is sufficiently limited to admit of treatment, which may make some claim to completeness, until fresh discoveries render additions or corrections necessary.

But, while thus limiting myself, I have not thought it necessary to remain absolutely silent about all the subsidiary coinages, and have permitted myself to make brief excursions into some adjacent fields, which are not included within the boundary of my plan.

The Mahârâjâs Gupta and Ghaṭotkacha, who occupy the first and second places in the dynastic list, seem not to have attained sufficiently high rank to warrant them in exercising the prerogative of coinage, and we need not expect ever to discover coins bearing their names. Certain gold coins were formerly attributed to Ghaṭotkacha, but erroneously.[2]

The numismatic record of the Imperial Gupta dynasty begins with the first 'sovereign of Mahârâjâs,' Chandra Gupta I., whose coinage is represented only by a few gold pieces of a single type. The scarcity of his coinage perhaps indicates a short reign.

His son and successor, Samudra Gupta, likewise, struck coins, so far as is known, in gold only, but his mint-masters issued them in at least six well-defined and distinct types.

The western extension of the Empire to Guzerât and Kâthiâwâṛ appears to have been the work of Chandra

[1] Guptas of Mahâ Kosala, or Central Provinces (*Arch. Rep.* vol. vii. p. vi; vol. xvii. pp. 17, 85, 87); of Orissa (*ibid.* vol. xvii. pp. 17, 85, 87); of Western Gauda, in Central Provinces (*ibid.* vol. ix. p. 156).

[2] See *post*, coins of Kâcha in Catalogue of Gold Coins, p. 74.

Gupta II., who issued a silver coinage based on that struck by the Satraps of Saurâshṭra in imitation of Græco-Bactrian hemidrachms. The extreme rarity of the silver coins of Chandra Gupta II., when contrasted with the abundant finds of the silver coinage of his successors, indicates that his silver mintage was small in amount and late in his reign. He also struck copper coins in his northern dominions of four types, three of which are very rare, while one is tolerably common. The gold coinage of Chandra Gupta II. occurs in at least eight different types. Most of these are scarce, and some are known only from unique specimens, but examples of the Archer type are sufficiently numerous to show that the issue of it must have been a very large one. The inscriptions, unfortunately, do not determine the initial date of the reign of Chandra Gupta II., and consequently we do not know its exact duration, but the number and variety of his extant coins warrant the inference that it was long.

The stone inscriptions and dated silver coins of Kumâra Gupta enable us to fix almost exactly the limits of his reign, which we know to have lasted about thirty-eight years. Several types of his silver coins have been discovered, and specimens of one type have been found in very large numbers. His copper coins are exceedingly rare, and only one or two specimens have yet been recognized. His gold coinage equals in variety of type that of his father, and examples of some forms of it are fairly abundant, though none can be called common.

The date of the conclusion of the reign of Skanda Gupta is not known with certainty, but he probably reigned for a period of twenty-five or nearly thirty years. His rude silver coins, which were struck in his western dominions, are numerous, but the better-executed coins in the same metal, which issued from his northern mints, appear to be rather scarce. One variety of his gold coinage has been found in considerable numbers, but the other forms are rare. His gold coinage is much less varied than that of his father and grandfather.

The coinage of Budha Gupta is known only from six specimens of a single type in silver. Of Toramâṇa we possess only two silver coins, but the copper coinage of his son Mihirakula is tolerably abundant. The silver coinage of Bhîma Sena and Krishṇa Râjâ is known from a few rare coins.[1]

The Later Guptas of Magadha seem to have coined only in gold, or base metal purporting to be gold, but their coinage has not been investigated with sufficient detail to enable me to indicate the rarity of their several issues. All, however, seem to be rather scarce.

Three examples are known of the silver coinage of Îśâna Varman, a member of the Maukhari dynasty of Western Magadha, but I do not know of any specimen of the gold coinage of this family.[2]

With this explanation of the limits which I have imposed on myself, I now proceed to the discussion of the coinage which I have undertaken to describe.

CHAPTER II.—TYPES AND DEVICES.

The Gupta gold coinage is remarkable for its great variety of type. The obverse devices are much more characteristic than the reverse ones, and necessarily form the primary basis for classification.

The gold coins, arranged according to their obverse devices, may be conveniently classified as follows :

Types of Gold Coins.

Reign.	*Type.*
Chandra Gupta I.	1. King and Queen. (Pl. I. 1.)
Samudra Gupta.	1. Tiger. (Pl. I. 2.)

[1] Brief notices of the coins of Bhîma Sena, Krishṇa Râjâ and Toramâṇa will be found *post* in the Supplement to my Catalogue of Silver Coins, pp. 135-138. No thorough account of the coins of Mihirakula has been published The B.M. possesses a good many specimens. See Ind. Ant. vol. xv. pp. 245-252, and 345-348.

[2] The coins of Îśâna Varmâ are noticed *post* in the Supplement to my Catalogue of Siver Coins, p. 136.

	2. Aśwamedha. (Pl. I. 4.)
	3. Lyrist. (Pl. I. 5, 6.)
	4. Javelin. (Pl. I. 7—9.)
	5. Archer. (Pl. I. 10.)
	6. Battle-axe. (Pl. I. 11, 12.)[1]
Kâcha (?=Samudra Gupta)	1. Standard. (Pl. I. 3.)[2]
Chandra Gupta II.	1. Couch. (Pl. I. 13.)
	2. Javelin. (Not figured.)
	3. Archer. (Pl. I. 14—16; Pl. II. 1, 2.)
	4. Horseman to Right. (Pl. II. 3.)[3]
	5. Horseman to Left. (Not figured.)
	6. Lion-Trampler. (Pl. II. 4.)
	7. Combatant Lion. (Pl. II. 5.)
	8. Retreating Lion. (Pl. II. 6.)
	9. Umbrella. (Pl. II. 7, 8.)[4]
Kumâra Gupta	1. Swordsman. (Pl. II. 9.)
	2. Archer. (Pl. II. 10—12.)
	3. Horseman to Right. (Pl. II. 13.)
	4. Horseman to Left. (Pl. II. 14.)
	5. Peacock. (Pl. III. 1, 2.)
	6. Lion Trampler. (Not figured.)
	7. Combatant Lion. (Pl. III. 3.)
	8. Two Queens. (Pl. III. 4.)
	9. Aśwamedha. (Pl. III. 5.)
Skanda Gupta.	1. King and Queen. (Pl. III. 6.)
	2. Archer. (Pl. III. 7, 8.)
Nara Bâlâditya.	Archer. (Pl. III. 11.)
Prakâśâditya.	Lion and Horseman. (Pl. III. 9, 10.)
Kramâditya.	Bull. (Pl. III. 12.)

The silver coins, unlike the gold, are all substantially identical in their obverse device, which consists of a conventional king's head, and their classification must rest, partly on the reverse devices, and partly on the legends. So classified, they fall into order as follows:

1 Formerly called by me Boy and Battle-axe.
2 Formerly named Solar Standard.
3 Formerly named Lancer.
4 Formerly called Swordsman and Umbrella.

Types of Silver Coins.

Reign.	*Type.*
Chandra Gupta II.	1. Vikramânka.
	2. Vikramâditya.
Kumâra Gupta.	1. Winged Peacock.
	2. Fantail Peacock.
	3. Trident.
Skanda Gupta.	1. Winged Peacock.
	2. Fantail Peacock.
	3. Bull.

The copper coins, like the gold, are readily distinguished by their obverse devices, and are classified as follows:

Types of Copper Coins.

Reign.	*Type.*
Chandra Gupta II.	1. Umbrella.
	2. Standing King.
	3. Vikramâditya Bust.
	4. Chandra Head.
Kumâra Gupta.	1. Standing King.
	? 2. Umbrella.

The reverse devices of the gold coins all agree in presenting as their main element the figure of a female, associated with emblems which prove that she is always intended to represent a divine personage, except perhaps in the case of the Aśwamedha medals of Samudra Gupta. The only exception to this statement is afforded by the newly-discovered Javelin type of Chandra Gupta II., the reverse device of which consists of the King and Queen seated on a couch, a design better suited for the obverse than for the reverse.

The reverse devices of the gold coins may be grouped as follows:

Class I.—Standing Goddess.

Device.	*Reign.*	*Type.*
1. Goddess holding lotus-flower in r., and cornucopiæ in l. hand.	Kâcha (?=Samudra Gupta).	Standard.

Device.	*Reign.*	*Type.*
2. Goddess holding fillet in r., and lotus-flower in l. hand (or fillet in r. hand only?)	Chandra Gupta II.	Umbrella.
3. Goddess holding fillet in r., and lotus-flower in l., and standing on a dragon.	Samudra Gupta.	Tiger.
	Chandra Gupta II.	? Umbrella.
4. ? Goddess, with fly-whisk.	Samudra Gupta.	Aśwamedha.
,, ,,	Kumâra Gupta.	,,
5. Goddess feeding peacock.	,, ,,	Combatant Lion.

Class II.—Seated Goddess.

1. Goddess seated on four-legged throne.	Samudra Gupta.	Javelin.
	,, ,,	Archer.
	Chandra Gupta II.	Couch.
	,, ,,	Archer, Class I.
2. Goddess seated cross-legged on open lotus-flower.	Chandra Gupta II.	Archer, Class II.
	Kumâra Gupta	Swordsman.
	,, ,,	Archer.
	,, ,,	Two Queens.
	Skanda Gupta	Archer.
	,, ,,	King and Queen.
	Nara Bâlâditya	Archer.
	Prakâśâditya	Lion and Horseman.
	Kramâditya	Bull.

Device.	*Reign.*	*Type.*
3. Goddess seated on wicker stool to l.		
a. Holding fillet and cornucopiæ.	Samudra Gupta.	Lyrist.
β. Holding fillet and lotus.	Chandra Gupta II.	Horseman to r.
	,, ,,	Horseman to l.
	Kumâra Gupta.	Horseman to r.
γ. Feeding peacock and holding lotus.	Kumâra Gupta.	Horseman to r.
	,, ,,	Horseman to l.
4. Goddess riding peacock.	Kumâra Gupta.	Peacock.
5. Goddess seated on back of couchant lion.		
a. Holding fillet and cornucopiæ.	Chandra Gupta I.	King and Queen.
β. Holding fillet and lotus, or fillet only, or lotus only.	Chandra Gupta II.	Lion-Trampler.
	,, ,,	Combatant Lion.
	,, ,,	Retreating Lion.
	Kumâra Gupta.	Lion-Trampler.

Class III.

King and Queen on couch.	Chandra Gupta II.	Javelin.

The reverse devices of the silver coins comprise :

Device.	*Reign.*	*Type.*
1. Winged peacock.	Chandra Gupta II.	Vikramânka.
	,, ,,	Vikramâditya.
	Kumâra Gupta.	Winged Peacock
	Skanda Gupta.	,, ,,

	Device.	*Reign.*	*Type.*
2.	Fantail Peacock.	Kumâra Gupta.	Fantail Peacock.
		Skanda Gupta.	,, ,,
		Budha Gupta.	,, ,,
		Toramâṇa, Bhîma Sena, and Îśâna Varmâ.	,, ,,
3.	Trident.	Kumâra Gupta.	Trident.
4.	Bull.	Skanda Gupta.	Bull.
	,,	Krishṇa Râjâ.	,,

The copper coins all exhibit the same reverse device, namely, a rude bird-like figure, with expanded wings, facing front, which appears to be intended for the mythical Garuḍa, the vehicle of Vishṇu.[1]

The reverse devices of all the Gupta coins, gold, silver, and copper, were in every case (except the Javelin type of Chandra Gupta II.) undoubtedly selected as being mythological symbols. The obverse devices are all, with the exception of those of the Aśwamedha medals, primarily representations, more or less conventional, of the several kings from whose mints the coins issued, but in some cases the die-artists evidently intended the obverse designs to have a mythological significance as well as those of the reverse.

I shall now proceed to discuss, as far as my limited knowledge permits, the meaning and origin of the great variety of devices enumerated above, dealing first with the gold coins.

The legends of the King and Queen coins of Chandra Gupta I. leave no doubt that the effigies on the obverse are primarily intended for the sovereign and his consort Kumâra Devî, a member of the Lichchhavi family. The queen's name is known from the stone inscriptions, as well as the coins. The king is figured leaning on a spear, and this device may be intended secondarily to symbolize Kumâra Deva, the god of war, and husband of Kumârî Devî. The reverse goddess seated on a lion is probably Durgâ, another form of Kumârî Devî, but the cornucopiæ in her left arm indicates that the deity is presented under her beneficent,

[1] Ind. Ant. vol. xiv. p. 93.

as well as her terrible aspect, and connects her with the image of Lakshmî, which is the commonest reverse device.

The device of the king and queen standing facing one another reappears in the coinage of Skanda Gupta, but in a modified form, and executed with inferior skill. The unique coin of Kumâra Gupta, which I have classed as the Two Queens type, presents the figure of the king standing between two females, and I can only suppose that the female figures are intended for his queens. It is quite certain that the central figure is the king, because he is labelled Kumâra Gupta, and it is therefore impossible to suppose that it is intended primarily for a god. It is, of course, possible that the device may have a secondary mythological signification. The attitude of the king on this coin suggested to Dr. Hoernlé a recollection of the conventional figure of Buddha,[1] but there is no reason whatever to suppose that any of the Gupta kings were Buddhists. Both inscriptions and coins, on the contrary, show clearly that they were Brahmanists. It is curious that the king of the Two Queens coin is smaller than either of the female figures. The male and female figures seated together on a couch on the reverse of the unique Javelin coin of Chandra Gupta II. appear intended for the king and his consort.

The obverse device of the Javelin coins of Samudra Gupta is obviously borrowed directly from that of the Indo-Scythian gold coins. It also bears a strong resemblance to the obverse of certain Macedonian coins. The figure on these latter coins has generally been described as that of a Roman emperor, but Professor Gardner prefers to regard it as an effigy of the god Ares (Mars).[2] I think that the design of the Gupta coins was influenced by that of the Macedonian. The device reappears on the unique Javelin coin of Chandra Gupta II.

In his Archer type Samudra Gupta substitutes for the javelin in the king's hand a bow, and the device thus

[1] Proc. A.S.B. Nov. 1883, p. 144.

[2] "Ares as a Sun-god, and Solar Symbols on the Coins of Macedon and Thrace," by Percy Gardner (*Num. Chron.* vol. xx. N.S. p. 56, pl. iv. fig. 4).

introduced long remained the favourite obverse pattern. It is found on the coins of Chandra Gupta II., Kumâra Gupta, and Skanda Gupta, and is the standard device of the barbarous gold coins of the obscure successors of the Imperial dynasty in the eastern provinces.

The device of the Archer coins may have been suggested by the Persian darics,[1] but this is not probable. If it had any symbolic meaning, it most likely was intended to suggest an analogy between the king who rules the earth and the sun that rules the heavens. The conception of the sun as an archer is familiar to poetry and mythology.

The unique Couch coin of Chandra Gupta II., which exhibits the king seated alone on a couch, with one leg tucked up under him, is copied from a common type of Indo-Scythian coins, and figures in the same attitude may be observed in the sculptures at Amarâvatî, dating from the close of the second century A.D.

The king of the rare Lyrist type of Samudra Gupta is seated in nearly the same attitude, but is engaged playing an Indian lyre (*viṇâ*). This device is clearly intended to commemorate the special accomplishments of Samudra Gupta, "who put to shame (Kâsyapa) the preceptor of (Indra) the lord of the gods, and Tumburu, and Nârada, and others, by (his) sharp and polished intellect, and choral skill and musical accomplishments; who established his title of 'king of poets' by various poetical compositions that were fit to be the means of subsistence of learned people." Nârada, with whom Samudra Gupta is compared, was the reputed inventor of the lyre.[2]

The Lyrist coins (Pl. I. 5), with the exception of the India Office specimen (Pl. I. 6), are broad, thin, medal-like pieces,

[1] I take this opportunity of remarking that an incidental reference of mine to Persian darics (J.A S.B. part i. vol. liii. p. 149) exaggerated the rarity of these coins. Sir A. Cunningham informs me that 300 were found in Xerxes' canal at Mount Athos, and that there is no reason to suppose that Warren Hastings was mistaken in describing as darics the 172 gold pieces found near Benares, which he sent home to the Court of Directors, and which speedily disappeared.

[2] Line 27 of the Allahabad Pillar inscription in *Corpus Inscr. Indic.* vol. iii. p 14, notes 1 and 2. Lines 6 and 16 of the same inscription also refer to the mental gifts of Samudra Gupta.

well-struck, and superior in execution to most of the Gupta coins.

The coins of the Aśwamedha type differ from all the other types by having on the obverse the figure of a horse instead of that of the king. The legend does not give the name of the king who struck them, but records that he had power to effect the Aśwamedha sacrifice. These coins can only be ascribed to Samudra Gupta, "who was the restorer of the Aśwamedha sacrifice, which had been long in abeyance."[1] The fact, known from the inscriptions, that Samudra Gupta actually did perform the sacrifice of the horse, which was incumbent on a claimant to the universal sovereignty of India, would alone suffice to justify the ascription to him of the Aśwamedha pieces; and the attribution is fully confirmed by the evidence yielded by the coins themselves, the legends of which are connected with those of the Javelin, Archer, and Lyrist types of Samudra Gupta. The syllable सि, 'Si,' which occurs on the exergue of both the Lyrist and Aśwamedha coins, has not yet been explained.[2]

I have no doubt that the Aśwamedha pieces were struck as medals to commemorate the successful performance of the horse sacrifice, and were distributed to the officiating Brahmans. The Bilsaṛ inscription expressly refers to Samudra Gupta as "the giver of millions of gold, performer of the Aśwamedha."[3] A coin of similar type, which seems to have been struck by Kumâra Gupta, is in the cabinet of Sir A. Cunningham (Pl. III. 5).

I do not know the meaning of the standard in front of the horse. Possibly it may be intended for the standard of Indra.[4]

The Tiger type of Samudra Gupta's coinage is known from a single coin only, which possesses considerable artistic merit. The king is shown armed with a bow, and trampling

[1] *Corpus. Inscr. Ind.* vol. iii. pp. 3, 4.

[2] Not 'Se,' as formerly read. It also occurs on a late Indo-Scythian coin from the Panjab in A. C. cabinet (*Ind. Ant.* vol. xiv. p. 94).

[3] *Ibid*, pp. 44, and 27, 28. I erroneously supposed formerly that the passage in the Bilsaṛ inscription referred to Kumâra Gupta.

[4] According to Mr. J. F. Hewitt, Indra "appears to be the special god of the warrior tribes, as opposed to the Brahmans" (J.R.A.S. Vol. XX. N.S. p. 335).

on a tiger which he is shooting in the mouth. The Combatant Lion and Lion Trampler types of Chandra Gupta II. and Kumâra Gupta are very similar in design. The unique Retreating Lion coin of Chandra Gupta II. presents another variation of the same conception, and is the most artistic piece in the Gupta coinage. It is possible that these lion and tiger obverses may have been suggested by Greek representations of Herakles contending with the Nemean lion, but I am not able to show any clear connection between the Greek and Indian designs. The Retreating Lion coin certainly has a Greek look, and I am persuaded that its spirited design was inspired by Western models.

The late coins of Prakâśâditya show a horseman attacking a lion or tiger, but the execution is degraded.

The goddess on the reverse of Samudra Gupta's Tiger type stands on a monster with an elephant's head and fish's tail. In mythology the fish-like dragon or *makara* is the vehicle of Varuṇa, the god of the waters. The king's name Samudra means the ocean, and I think it almost certain that the obverse device idealizes Samudra Gupta as Varuṇa, while the reverse represents the sea-god's consort.[1] The Allâhâbâd Pillar inscription compares Samudra Gupta with Dhanada or Kuvera, the god of wealth, Varuṇa, the god of the waters, Indra, the god of the sky, and Antaka or Yama, the god of death.

The Battle-axe coins, which present Samudra Gupta as a warrior grasping a battle-axe and describe him as "armed with the axe of Kṛitânta" or Yama, obviously are intended to express visibly the comparison with the god of death, which the inscription makes in words. The epithet "armed with the axe of Kṛitânta" is also applied in the inscriptions to Samudra Gupta.

The king of the Standard type of Kâcha appears to be unarmed. The standard which he supports bears a rayed emblem, which may symbolize the sun, and reappears on the Wheel variety of the Archer type of Chandra Gupta II. The

[1] *Cf.* the introduction of Demeter in the coins of Demetrius of Syria. Monsters like that on which the coin goddess stands are not uncommon in early Indian sculpture.

style of the Standard coins closely approximates to that of the undoubted coins of Samudra, and I agree with Mr. Fleet in thinking it probable that Kâcha was a title or second name of Samudra Gupta. These coins were formerly attributed erroneously to Ghaṭotkacha, the second Mahârâjâ of the Gupta Dynasty.

The Horseman types are confined to the reigns of Chandra Gupta II. and his son Kumâra Gupta of the Imperial Dynasty, and the coins of both princes show the royal horseman turned both to left and right. He is sometimes armed with a bow. The Bactrian coinage offers many examples of equestrian portraits, which were probably the patterns imitated by the mint-masters of the Gupta Kings. The figure of a horseman also appears on the coins of the king who took the title of Prakâśâditya.

Chandra Gupta II., as depicted on his Umbrella gold coins, is armed with a sword, and shaded by an umbrella, carried by an attendant. The device of the Umbrella copper coins of the same reign is similar, but the execution is much ruder than that of the gold coins. The legend of the latter and the king's weapon connect them with the Swordsman coins of Kumâra Gupta.

The peacock is the special emblem of the war-god Kumâra (or Kârttikeya) and his consort Kumârî Devî, and is naturally prominent on the coins of Kumâra Gupta.[1] It is not, however, peculiar to his coinage. His gold coins of the Peacock type on the obverse depict the king offering fruit to a peacock, and on the reverse show the goddess Kumârî Devî riding on her sacred bird. The execution of some of these coins is very delicate, and the plate does not do them full justice. The goddess on the reverse of Kumâra Gupta's Combatant Lion gold coins is standing feeding a peacock, and on the reverse of his Horseman coins is seated on a wicker stool, performing the same act. I presume that in

[1] *Cf.* the mention of the later Kumâra Gupta in l. 5 of the Aphsaṛ inscription of Âditya Sena—"That king begat one son, by name the illustrious Kumâra Gupta, of renowned strength, a leader in battle; just as (the god) Hara begat a son (Kârttikeya), who rides upon the peacock."—*Corpus Inscr. Ind.* vol. iii. p. 206.

all cases the goddess associated with the peacock is intended for Kumârî Devî.

The Fantail Peacock types of the silver coinage of Kumâra Gupta, Skanda Gupta, and Budha Gupta exhibit a peacock with expanded tail in the same attitude as on the variety β coins of Kumâra's gold Peacock type. An exact prototype of this design may be seen on the reverse of a coin of Julia Augusta, a daughter of Titus, who died between A.D. 81 and 90.[1] Kumâra Gupta flourished between the years A.D. 414 and 452, and the interval of time between him and Julia Augusta is very considerable. But the resemblance between his coins and hers is so great that I do not think it can be accidental. We know that Roman coins were familiar objects in India during the early centuries of the Christian era. A coin of Paulina (A.D. 217-228) is also very similar in its treatment of the peacock to the Gupta coins. Coins of Mariniana (*circa* A.D. 250) and of Manlia Scantilla Augusta (A.D. 193) may also be compared.[2] I have no doubt that the Gupta representations of Kumârî Devî and the peacock are Hinduized adaptations of some or other of the devices of the Roman coins which bear representations of the peacock in association with the goddess Juno, or a deified lady of the imperial house.

The silver coins of Chandra Gupta II., Kumâra Gupta, and Skanda Gupta, which I have classed as the Winged Peacock types, have a very ill-executed, and sometimes very obscure, reverse device, which has been variously interpreted as a peacock standing to front, as a goddess, and as an altar. This device, as seen on many specimens, is certainly intended as a rough diagram of a bird, and the bird is presumably a peacock. As shown on many coins of Skanda Gupta, the device is not in the least like a bird. But the history of coins offers so many examples of degradations of design that I am willing to believe, till some better explanation is found, that in all cases the obscure device in question is intended for a bird, that is to say, a peacock. This is the opinion of

[1] Trésor de Numismatique, Iconographie des Empereurs Romains, pl. xxii. 11.
[2] *Ibid.* plates xlviii. 4, 5; lii. 3; xli. 1.

Sir A. Cunningham, whose unrivalled knowledge of Hindu coins gives special weight to his judgment on a question of the sort. It is not, however, easy to understand why both correct and unrecognizable delineations of the same bird should be minted by one sovereign. The only available explanation is afforded by the fact that the coins with the well-drawn peacock appear to have been minted in Northern India, and that those with the unrecognizable device were the coinage of Guzerât and Kâṭhiâwâr.

On the Javelin gold coins of Samudra Gupta, the Swordsman coins of Kumâra Gupta, and the Archer types of Samudra Gupta, Chandra Gupta II., Kumâra Gupta, and Skanda Gupta, the king's arm is extended across a standard surmounted by a bird facing front.

The bird on the standard is necessarily designed on a very small scale, and shows no details, but, so far as it can be seen, it has a general resemblance to the bird-like creature on the reverse of the copper coins of Chandra Gupta II. and Kumâra, and is not altogether unlike the object on the reverse of some of the Winged Peacock silver coins. The copper coins are rudely executed, and in the case of most of them it is hard to say what the creature on the reverse is intended for. The Hindu die-cutters were very ready to make use of foreign designs and adapt them to the use of their own mythology. It is, therefore, quite possible that, as suggested by Professor Gardner, the reverse device of the copper coins may have been suggested by the owl of Athênê as seen on the coins of Pergamon. One specimen of the Umbrella type in the possession of Sir A. Cunningham (Pl. IV. 9) plainly delineates, in addition to the expanded wings, appendages which seem to be intended for human arms, and a few other specimens afford less distinct indications of the same intention. I do not think that the bird on the copper coins can be intended for a peacock, which it does not in the least resemble. Its head is drawn nearly circular, and was probably intended to represent a human face. For these reasons I now agree with Mr. Fleet in regarding the bird on the copper coins as a representation of Garuḍa, the monster, half-man, half-bird, on which Vishṇu is believed to ride.[1] But the device may have been suggested by Greek coins, and given a Hindu signification.

It is impossible to be quite certain what was meant by the bird on the standard of the gold coins, but the fact that the Allâhâbâd Pillar inscription mentions 'Garuḍa tokens' (*Garutmatanka*) or standards, renders it probable that the bird on the standard also was intended for Garuḍa.[2] I have no doubt that, whatever its meaning as a Hindu symbol, the form of the bird-standard was copied from the eagle of the Roman *aurei*, which were probably re-struck as Gupta *dînârs*.[3]

The goddess seated on a wicker stool and turned to the left is found, with variation in the accessories, on the Lyrist type of Samudra Gupta, and on the Horseman types, both Right and Left, of Chandra Gupta II. and Kumâra Gupta. Her attributes on the coins of Samudra Gupta and Chandra Gupta II. indicate that she is intended to represent a form of Lakshmî or Good Fortune; her association with the peacock on the coins of Kumâra Gupta suggests that she is there intended also as a representation of Kumârî Devî. The design itself is undoubtedly of foreign origin. The goddess of the Gupta coins seated on the wicker stool is almost an exact copy of Demeter as represented on a rare coin of the island of Paros in the British Museum, and the resemblance is so close that both designs must be referred to a common source.

The device of the Gupta coins may have been directly imitated from that of Apollo seated on the ὄμφαλος, with its cover of the ἄγρηνον net, as seen on the Seleucid coins of Syria.[4] Seleucid coins are sometimes found in India, and the devices of Apollo on the Syrian, and of Demeter on the Parian coins, are certainly connected with one another.

[1] Ind. Ant. vol. xiv. p. 93.

[2] Corpus Inscr. Ind. vol. iii. p. 14, *note* 3.

[3] The word *dînâr* is used in Gupta inscriptions for a gold coin. The Gaṛhwâ (Gaḍhwâ) inscription from the Allahabad district is remarkable for expressing certain endowments both in *dînâras* and *suvarṇas* (*Corpus Inscr. Ind.* vol. iii. p. 266, No. 64).

[4] *Cf.* the coins of Antiochus I. (J.A.S.B. vol. l. part i. p. 178, pl. xviii. 14, 15).

The standing king engaged in sacrificing at a small altar, who appears on the obverse of so many of the Gupta gold coins, is obviously an adaptation of the corresponding figure on many coins of Kanerki (Kanishka) and other Indo-Scythian princes. The altar is found on the Javelin coins of Samudra Gupta, the Archer type, variety β of the same prince, the coins of Kâcha, the Umbrella type of Chandra Gupta II., and the Swordsman type of Kumâra Gupta. On later coins the king, instead of sacrificing at an altar, holds an arrow in his hand.

The reverse goddess of the gold coins, whether standing, or seated on a throne, or on an open lotus-flower, or on a lion, or on a wicker stool, is frequently represented as holding a cornucopiæ. Mr. Theobald has devoted much pains to an attempt to prove that the object which I call a cornucopiæ is really intended to represent a many-headed Nâga, or sacred snake.[1] It is true that on some coins the symbol does recall to mind the polycephalic Nâga which is familiar in the sculptures of Amarâvatî and elsewhere, and it is possible, or even probable, that the Hindus who cut the Gupta dies were conscious that the symbol they engraved suggested the sacred snake.

But I think it is perfectly plain that the symbol in question was primarily a horn of plenty, copied from the Indo-Scythian coins, and, indirectly, either from the Syrian or Roman coins. The cornucopiæ symbol appears for the last time on the rare coins forming Class I. of the Archer type of Chandra Gupta II., which were probably struck early in his reign, and must be dated about A.D. 400.[2]

The presence of the horn of plenty symbol shows that the goddess, whether sitting or standing, who holds it, is intended to be presented in a beneficent aspect. When she holds the cornucopiæ and is seated on a lion, as in the case of the coins of Chandra Gupta I., it is obvious that the symbolism is intended to suggest both the terrible and the beneficent

[1] J.A.S.B. vol. liv. part i. pp. 84–92.

[2] In illustration of the fact that the cornucopiæ was a foreign symbol I may mention that in M. Williams' English-Sanskrit Dictionary the word has to be rendered by a long periphrasis. No Sanskrit name for the symbol is adduced.

aspects of the goddess, and it is immaterial whether we call her Pârvatî, or Durgâ, or Lakshmî, for she partakes of the special characteristics of each.

The goddess seated on a four-legged throne, who appears on the reverse of the Javelin and Archer types of Samudra Gupta, and the Couch and Class I. Archer types of the early part of the reign of Chandra Gupta II., is unmistakeably an adaptation of the goddess who is named ΑΡΔΟΧΡΟ, 'Ardochro,' on the Indo-Scythian coins. The coins of Class II. Archer type of Chandra Gupta II. introduce the reverse device of a goddess seated on an open lotus-flower, which remained for some centuries the standard design for the reverse of gold and copper coins in Northern India. This device seems not to have differed substantially from that of the throne-seated goddess in symbolical meaning, and the devices of the goddess standing, or seated on a wicker stool, unless when differentiated by special symbols, appear to have had the same general signification. These goddesses commonly, though not always, carry a lotus-flower in one hand, and a noose or fillet (*pâśa*) in the other. They agree in the main with the description of the goddess Srî or Lakshmî, consort of Vishṇu. "She is the goddess of good luck and plenty. . . She is worshipped by filling the corn-measure with wheat or other grain, and thereon placing flowers. She is represented as a lovely and benign woman, clothed in yellow, holding a lotus in her hand, and seated on a lotus, or beside Vishṇu. Sometimes, as is likewise Vishṇu, she is painted all yellow, and has four arms, and she holds in one of her right arms a rosary, and the *pâśa* or cord in one of her left. This cord is seen also in the hands of Varuṇa and Śiva, and is emblematical of the sea, which girds the earth."[1] In Sanskrit poetry Lakshmî is described as *ambujâsinâ*, or seated on the lotus.[2] The following description of her attributes by Sir Monier Williams will further elucidate the symbolism of the coins. "Lakshmî—the goddess of fortune or prosperity, wife of the god Vishṇu. She is said also to preside over

[1] Birdwood, Industrial Arts of India, vol. i. p. 58.
[2] I am indebted to Mr. E. J. Rapson for the quotation of this epithet.

beauty, and, in this respect, as well as in the story of her birth, agrees in character with Venus. She was born, according to the usual accounts, from the ocean, when churned by the gods and Asuras, and emerged from the foam of the sea, seated on a full-blown lotus, and holding a lotus in her hand. Her countenance is represented as incomparably beautiful. As presiding over abundance she resembles Ceres. . . . . As seated on, or holding, the lotus, or as identified with this flower, which is the symbol of prosperity, पद्मा, कमला, पद्मालया, पद्मवासा, पद्मस्नुषा . . . As mother of Kâmadeva, माया . . . . As mother of the world, लोकमाता, माता." [1]

I have, therefore, no doubt that the goddess, who is seated on a throne in Samudra's coins, on a lotus-flower in the coins of Chandra Gupta II. and his successors, and also (in certain cases) the goddess seated on a wicker stool, or standing, are all intended to express substantially the same conception, that of the benign and kindly Good Fortune, the bestower of happiness and plenty, the consort of the wise ruler; the same who was named Τύχη and Demeter by the Greeks, Fortuna, Ceres, Abundantia, etc., by the Romans, and Ardochro by the Indo-Scythians.

Sir Alexander Cunningham is of opinion that the Indo-Scythian Ardochro "represents the Earth, the *Alma Venus* of Lucretius, and the mother of all things, *μήτηρ πάντων*, as Euripides calls her." [2] Dr. Von Sallet remarks that "the goddess Ardochro, who appears on the Turushka coins up to the latest times, is identical with Demeter. She is an exact repetition of the sitting Demeter with cornucopiæ and ears of corn on the coins of Azes—that is to say, of the sitting Demeter only. The standing Demeter also holds the cornucopiæ, and is of course identical with the sitting form. This remark is by no means superfluous. The identity of the sitting and the standing Ardochro must be insisted on for the reason that it happens elsewhere in the case of these

[1] M. Williams, English-Sanskrit Dictionary, *s.v.* Lakshmî.
[2] Babylonian and Oriental Record, vol. ii. p. 43.

coins that the same name appears along with quite distinct figures. For instance, the name Athro is found on coins of king Ooerki along with the figure of Hephaistos, and on other coins of the Turushka kings along with that of a bearded warrior, who holds in his hand a sword, as well as a garland or diadem."[1]

The noose or fillet (*pâśa*), so often seen in the right hand of the goddess on the reverse of the gold coins has been mentioned above as one of the common accessories of the representations of Lakshmî and other deities. This emblem on the Gupta coins is, as explained by Mr. Theobald, of ambiguous meaning.[2] On the one hand, it is connected with the classic *vitta* or fillet, the emblem both of purity and power, and, on the other, with the Hindu noose symbol, which appears to have symbolized many things. As drawn on the Gupta gold coins the emblem is more of a noose than a fillet. It does not matter much which name is applied to it, and I shall continue to use the name fillet, subject to the foregoing remarks.

The gold coins, as has been shown, present a remarkable variety of obverse types. The silver coins, on the other hand, though readily distinguishable into groups by differences in their legends or reverse devices, have all substantially the same obverse device, namely, that of the king's head turned to the right, wearing a low cap or helmet. Many pieces exhibit a defective and corrupt legend in unintelligible Greek characters, which seem intended to stand for the PAO NANO PAO of the Indo-Scythian coinage. The Fantail Peacock coins of Kumâra Gupta, Skanda Gupta, and Budha Gupta are dated in the old Indian numerals, which were in use before the introduction of the present notation. On the coins of Toramâṇa, who belonged to a different dynasty, and succeeded Budha Gupta in Western India, the king's head is turned to the left.[3]

[1] Translated from p. 230 of Die Nachfolger Alexanders des Grossen in Baktrien und Indien, von Alfred von Sallet, Berlin, 1879.

[2] J.A.S.B. vol. liv. part i. p 85.

[3] Cunningham, Arch. Rep. vol. ix. p. 26; and Fleet, Corpus Inscrip. Indic. vol. iii. p. 11. Both Chandra Gupta and Kumâra Gupta indifferently turn their

The reverse devices of the silver coins have been enumerated above, and the derivation of the Fantail Peacock device has been explained. The obscure device, which I call the Winged Peacock, is barbarous in execution, and it is impossible to trace its origin more particularly. The Trident type connects the coins of Kumâra Gupta with those of the later Senapati Bhaṭârka of Valabhi, and the recumbent bull of the Bull type of Skanda Gupta's coinage was the special emblem of the kings of Valabhi, who succeeded the Guptas in Kaṭhiâwâṛ, and continued to use the same era. It is also found on the Nâga coins of Narwâr.[1]

The obverse device and the general style of the Gupta silver coins are obviously copied from the coins of the Satraps of Saurâshtra, whom the Gupta kings supplanted. The clusters of dots on some of the Gupta coins represent the rayed sun of the early Satrap coins.[2]

The Satrap coins are imitations of Greek *hemidrachmæ*, and bear a considerable resemblance to the coins of the Bactrian king Kodes.

I have already referred to the Umbrella type of the copper coinage. The Standing King obverse device is also connected with the gold coinage. The bust of the king, with a flower in his right hand, of the Vikramâditya Bust type, is a rude imitation of well-known gold coins of Ooerki (Huvishka).

The reverse device of the copper coins has been explained above.

CHAPTER III.—MONOGRAMMATIC EMBLEMS.

The so-called monograms occur on the reverse of the Gupta gold coins, in the left field, over the right shoulder of the goddess.

Horseman devices right and left. I doubt, therefore, whether any significance can be attached to the fact that the head on Toramâṇa's coins is turned to the left.

[1] Cunningham, Arch. Rep. vol. ix. pp. 23, 31.

[2] J.Bo.R.A.S. vol. vii. p. 23 (1862). The reference is to Mr. Newton's paper 'On the Sâh, Gupta, and other Ancient Dynasties of Kattiâwâr and Guzerat,' which gives a very careful account of the Satrap coins, with a plate. The Satraps used erroneously to be called the Sâh Dynasty, owing to a misreading of the cognomen Siṅha. See also Mr. Newton's paper 'On Recent Additions to our Knowledge of the Ancient Dynasties of Western India,' in Bo.J.R.A.S. vol. ix. p. 1 (1868).

I have observed only one certain instance where a monogram is found on both obverse and reverse, namely, a coin of the Javelin type of Samudra Gupta, No. 688 of the Bodleian collection, which has monogram 6*a* on the reverse, and a variety of monogram 19 on the obverse. The obverse emblem looks as if it had been twice struck.

The forms assumed by the monogrammatic emblems on the numerous gold coins which I have examined are shown in Plate V. The most common forms consist of a horizontal line, or two parallel horizontal lines, surmounted by either three or four dots or short prongs, and having a square or lozenge attached below by one corner.

Sometimes the square or lozenge is replaced by a cross, and sometimes by other devices, and occasionally the prongs or dots above the horizontal line are wanting. One form (No. 25), which I know only from a drawing, and for the accuracy of which I cannot answer, departs altogether from the standard pattern.

Examination of the plate will show the large variety of minor modifications in detail which occur.

The following statement exhibits the monograms which have come under my observation, arranged according to reigns:

Reign.	*Monogram.*
Chandra Gupta I.	3*a*; 4*a*; 4*b*; 5; 8*d*; 22*b*.
Samudra Gupta.	3*a*; 4*b*; 4*c*; 4*d*; 6*a*; 6*b*; 8*a*; 8*b*; 9; 11; 19*a*; 19*c*; 20*a*; 20*b*; 21; 22*a*; 22*b*.
Kâcha (?=Samudra Gupta.)	1; 2*a*; 2*b*; 4*a*.
Chandra Gupta II.	3*a*; 3*b*; 3*d*; 4*c*; 4*e*; 7*a*; 7*b*; 8*a*; 8*b*; 10*a*; 10*b*; 10*c*; 12; 15; 16; 17*a*; 17*b*; 17*c*; 18; 19*a*; 19*b*; 19*d*; 19*e*; 20*a*; 21; 22; 23; 24.
Kumâra Gupta.	3*b*; 8*a*; 8*b*; 8*c*; 10*c*; 17*c*; 17*d*; 19*b*; 20*a*; 25.
Skanda Gupta.	3*a*; 3*b*; 4*c*?; 8*a*.
Heavy coins of Chandra, etc.	8*a*; 8*e*; 10*a*; 13; 14; 19*a*.

The following types have no monogram :

Reign.	*Type.*
Samudra Gupta.	Aśwamedha.
,, ,,	Tiger.
Chandra Gupta II.	Javelin.
Kumâra Gupta.	Horseman to Left.
,, ,,	Peacock.
,, ,,	Aśwamedha.

In the following types the monogram is sometimes present, and sometimes wanting :

Reign.	*Type.*
Samudra Gupta.	Lyrist.
Chandra Gupta II.	Horseman to Right.
,, ,,	Horseman to Left.
,, ,,	Lion-Trampler.
,, ,,	Umbrella.
Kumâra Gupta.	Horseman to Right.[1]

Monogrammatic emblems do not occur either on the silver or copper coins.[2]

The foregoing lists teach us that the monogram, though usually inserted, was frequently omitted, and was not considered indispensable.

The so-called monograms on the Gupta coins correspond to the similar emblems on the Indo-Scythian coinage, and whatever explanation applies to those of the one series necessarily applies to those of the other.

The general type of the Indo-Scythian and Gupta monograms is one, but the details vary, and I doubt if a single example of the Indo-Scythian series is exactly reproduced on a Gupta coin. A comparison of Wilson's plate of the Indo-Scythian monograms in the Ariana Antiqua with my Plate of the corresponding Gupta emblems will prove the correctness of this assertion.

[1] The above lists differ considerably from those given in J.A.S.B. vol. liii. part i. pp. 137, 138, subsequent discoveries and observations having rendered correction necessary.

[2] A mark like an iota occurs commonly on the coins of the Satraps of Saurâshtra before the date, and occasionally on the Gupta silver coins, which Mr. Newton supposed to be a mint-mark.

Real monograms, combinations of letters, usually Greek, occur on the field of the Græco-Bactrian coinage, some of which are certainly the names or initials of mint-cities. The analogy of the Bactrian coins has led to the application of the name monogram to the corresponding marks on the Indo-Scythian and Gupta mintages, but, strictly speaking, the name is not applicable in either case. The so-called Indo-Scythian and Gupta monograms are not combinations of letters of any alphabet. They have sometimes been called emblems, but that word is inconveniently vague, and the term monogrammatic emblem is cumbrous. I therefore use the name monogram as a convenient abbreviation, and hope that this explanation will prevent any misunderstanding of my meaning.

In my essay on the gold coins I expressed a hope that the precise significance of the Gupta monograms might be elucidated, but so far this hope has not been realized. They are certainly not the marks of individual mint-masters or other functionaries, because the same monogram runs on from reign to reign through a period exceeding a century in duration.

With equal certainty it may be affirmed that they are not blundered copies of the Indo-Scythian monograms. The Gupta coins, though closely related to the Indo-Scythian mintages, are not in any respect blind imitations of them, and are characterized by much originality of design, nor are the Gupta monograms inferior in mechanical execution to the Indo-Scythian, from which they differ with systematic, and obviously intentional, variety. The Gupta and Indo-Scythian die-cutters certainly meant to express substantially the same ideas by their monograms, but one did not copy from the other.

I am convinced that the Gupta monograms do not indicate the mint-cities. The Indo-Scythian dominion in India began in, and spread from the Panjâb, and continued to exist there at least as late as the time of Samudra Gupta. There is no reason to suppose that the Guptas ever held the Panjâb, in which province none of their remains are found. Yet, as

I have observed, the general similarity between the Indo-Scythian and Gupta monograms is obvious, and it is incredible that marks so nearly alike should be used to indicate Indo-Scythian mints in the Panjâb, and also mints in Bihâr and the adjoining provinces, where the Gupta gold coins appear to have been struck.

We find further that Gupta coins found together in a single hoard, and therefore presumably minted in one province, exhibit many monograms. Thirty-two coins of the Bharsar hoard present five monograms among twenty-five coins, and seven pieces had no monogram at all. Other hoards which I have examined present the same phenomenon.

The description of Types and Devices in the preceding chapter will have satisfied the reader that mythological symbolism is characteristic of the Gupta coins, as it is of the Indo-Scythian, and all ancient coinages. The presumption therefore is that the monograms are in harmony with the rest of the design, and have a religious or mythological significance, and I am convinced that, in general terms, this explanation of their meaning is the correct one.

But I cannot profess to explain them in detail. In my former publication I noted the curiously close likeness between monogram *6a*, and the Egyptian symbol for the bee, which is said to have been the sign royal in the Hieratic character, and observed that a trident, which bears a resemblance to some of the Indo-Scythian and Gupta monograms, occurs, detached like them, in the field of a coin of Rhescuporis II., King of the Bosporos (A.D. 17 to 34). The four-pronged symbol in the hand of ? Victory on some coins of Azes is identical with the upper part of many of the Indo-Scythian and Gupta monograms.[1] I attach no importance to these observations, and repeat them merely on the chance that they may suggest a clue to a detailed interpretation.

Subsequent investigation has enabled me to contribute little more to the elucidation of the problem, but I have noticed that certain marks called by Mr. Thomas "harrows" and "trees," which occur on some of the early punch-

[1] Gardner, Greek and Scythic Kings of Bactria and India, pl. xviii. 11.

marked Indian coins of uncertain date, bear a general resemblance to the pronged forms of the Indo-Scythian and Gupta monograms.[1] I think it is not unlikely that these pronged forms are connected with the familiar trident or *triśûl* emblem, which was used as a symbol by different religions in many different senses, and that they are thus connected with symbols of almost world-wide use. At present I am unable to make any further suggestion, and can only renew the expression of the hope that the puzzle of the Indo-Scythian and Gupta "monograms" will eventually be solved.

Chapter IV.—Legends.

In order to present a detailed account of the palæography of the Gupta coins it would be necessary to give a plate of alphabets, which would be costly and troublesome to prepare, and would scarcely repay the trouble.[2] It may, however, be worth while to note, in an unsystematic way, a few peculiarities in the forms of the alphabet which occur in the coin legends, and to examine briefly the legends themselves.

The most remarkable peculiarity in the forms of characters used is the omission of the upper vowel marks in the Western series of silver coins. The Northern issues of the silver coinage with the reverse device of a peacock with expanded tail bear legends with the vowel marks above the line fully indicated. This distinction was first noted by Mr. Fleet, and my examination of the coins fully confirms its existence. Plate IV. Fig. 2 shows that the omission of the vowel marks in the Western series was intentional, and not due to want of room on the coin. The coin there figured retains the dotted circle outside the legend, but the vowel marks are wanting, just as they are in coins where the legend is close to the margin. The practice of omitting the vowel marks also

[1] J.A S.B. vol. xxxiv. part i. pl. xi. nos. 10 and 14. The same plate was also published in *Numism. Chron.* N.S. vol. iv. pl. xi.

[2] A valuable table of alphabets, including the characters of some of the Satrap and Gupta inscriptions, is given in plate v. of vol. iv. of the Archæological Survey of Western India.

obtains in the coinage of the Satraps of Saurâshṭra, the model of the Gupta silver coinage. The vowel marks are omitted in the legends of a few of the gold coins, but, as a rule, they are inserted.

The form of the letter *m* presents remarkable variations. Coins of Samudra Gupta frequently present on the same piece this letter both in a slightly modified form of the character in the Aśoka alphabet (No. 1), and in the square form with an indentation in the left limb, which is most common in the Gupta inscriptions (No. 2). The letter also frequently takes the form of two lines meeting in a point resting on a horizontal line (No. 3). A silver coin of Skanda Gupta in the British Museum twice renders medial *m* by three dots, arranged in a triangle with the apex at the bottom (No. 5), and another silver coin of the same king renders medial *m* by a single dot (No. 6). On a gold coin of Samudra Gupta in the Bodleian cabinet *m* assumes a square form without any indentation (No. 4). The following are the principal forms of *m* :

(1) X ; (2) ΣJ ; (3) V ; (4) ㄩ ; (5) ∵ ; (6) .

The *p*, *t*, *h*, and *y* also display considerable variations of form, and there is hardly any letter in the alphabet which does not vary perceptibly in shape.

The unique Standing King copper coin of Kumâra Gupta in the Bodleian collection is remarkable for expressing long *â* by a vertical stroke behind the *m*, as in the modern alphabet (*post*, p. 143). All other coins which I have seen express this vowel, when it is expressed at all, by a mark above the line, generally turned towards the right.

The nasal in the word Siṅha is always written as the guttural nasal, and not as *anuswâra*.

The *k* in Vikrama on the coins of Chandra Gupta II. is frequently doubled.[1]

The characters for *cha* and *ndra* on the rare silver Vikramâditya coins of Chandra Gupta II. are so peculiar

1 In inscriptions of the Gupta period *t* and *k*, when followed by *r*, are often doubled, *e.g.* the Asîrgaṛh seal of Sarvavarman (*Corpus Inscr. Ind.* vol. iii. p. 20).

in shape that they were read as Bakra instead of Chandra by Mr. Newton and Sir E. C. Bayley, but the right reading is undoubtedly Chandra.

On some silver coins of Skanda Gupta the *k* in the conjunct character *ska* is rendered by a loop, which looks like a *v*.

The letters forming the king's name in the field on the obverse of the gold coins are arranged vertically, and must be read from top to bottom. The arrangement of the letters of the name Kumâra Gupta on the unique Two Queens coin is most peculiar. The letters lie on their side, but the word Kumâra, on the right of the central figure, is to be read from above, and the word Gupta, on the left, from below (Plate III. 4).

The legends on the silver coins of Skanda Kramâditya are extremely rude and irregular.

The legends of the Gupta coins consist of the kings' names with the addition of various boastful titles or epithets and laudatory phrases. The queen's name is also recorded on one type, and will probably be found on one or two other types when better specimens than those now available come to light.

Chandra Gupta I. in the single known type of his coinage contented himself with the record of his own and his consort's names, and the addition of the word 'Lichchhavayaḥ' (the Lichchhavis), intimating that his queen belonged to the Lichchhavi royal family of Nepâl. It is evident that he was very proud of this alliance. He abstains from the use of bragging phrases.

His successor, Samudra Gupta, was fond of titles, and of vaunting his conquests, prowess, and accomplishments. We know his coinage in gold only. I presume that his Tiger type, preserved in a single specimen, was his earliest coinage, because he there assumes the plain title of Râjâ only. On the obverse he describes himself as *vyâghra parâkrama* (? or *vikrama*), 'equal in might to the tiger,' and on the reverse simply as *Râjâ Samudra Gupta*. Possibly the coins of this type may have been struck during his father's lifetime. The Tiger, Aśwamedha, and Lyrist types of Samudra are connected by the circumstance that all three look more like medals than ordinary coins. The Tiger and Aśwamedha coins agree in having standing goddesses on the reverse, and the Lyrist and Aśwamedha types are related by their common possession of the mysterious syllable 'Si' in a detached position in the exergue.

Samudra Gupta had a special liking for the word *parâkrama*, 'power' or 'might.' The obverse legend of the Aśwamedha pieces is imperfect, but contains a boast of having conquered the earth (*pṛithivî*); the reverse records the fact that the king had power to celebrate the horse sacrifice (*Aśwamedha parâkrama*).

The Lyrist type on the reverse simply gives the king's name, which is repeated on the obverse with the addition of the prefix *Śrî*, and the sovereign title of *Mahârâjâdhirâjâ*.

The Javelin type on the obverse has a long legend stating that "his majesty (*deva*), having conquered [the earth], and being victor in a hundred battles of various kinds, is victorious." The reverse bears the word *parâkrama*, 'might' or 'prowess,' alone.

One variety of Samudra's Archer type repeats *parâkrama* as the sole reverse legend, the other substitutes the epithet *apratiratha*, 'invincible in his war-chariot,' which is also used in the inscriptions to characterize Samudra Gupta. The obverse legend seems to be of the same purport as that of the Javelin type, the synonym *kshiti* being substituted for *pṛithivî*, 'earth.'

The legends of the Battle-axe type explain the symbolism of the devices, and compare the king to Yama, god of Death and Judgment, under his name of *Kṛitânta*, 'he that maketh an end.' The obverse also gives the king the title of *Râjâdhirâjâ*, and not the higher title of *Mahârâjâdhirâjâ* which is used on the Lyrist coin.

The style and reverse device plainly connect the coins of Kâcha with the Tiger and Aśwamedha types of Samudra Gupta, of whom Kâcha was probably a title. These coins bear the remarkable legend *Kâcho gâm avajitya karmabhir uttamair jayati*, 'Kâcho, having vanquished the earth, by excellent deeds is victorious,' and the king is called 'the exterminator of all râjâs,' an epithet applied in four, or perhaps five, inscriptions to Samudra Gupta.[1]

The correct *sandhi*, or euphonic change of vowels and consonants, in this legend and the legends of some other northern Gupta coins is noticeable.

The epithet *deva*, 'divine,' which Mr. Fleet renders by 'his majesty,' first appears on Samudra's Javelin pieces. It reappears on the unique Couch coin of Chandra Gupta II., and on several later issues, both gold and silver.

Chandra Gupta II. affected the use of the word *vikrama*, instead of the synonymous *parâkrama*, which Samudra Gupta preferred, and sometimes used the compound epithets *vikramâditya* 'sun of power,' and *vikramânka* 'arm of power.' The latter epithet occurs on the silver coins only. The title *vikramâditya* is found on the gold, silver, and copper coins of Chandra Gupta II.

Ordinarily the personal title used by one Gupta king is not used by another, but the title *Vikramâditya* is undoubtedly used on ten rude silver coins in the British Museum which bear the name of Skanda Gupta.

The special appellation of Skanda Gupta was *Kramâditya*, a synonym of *Vikramâditya*, which occurs on both the Winged Peacock (Altar) and Bull types of his silver coinage, and on his heavy gold coins of the *suvarṇa* standard. The gold coins of Kumâra with the title of *Kramâditya* (Arch. Rep. vol. xvi. p. 81) appear to belong to the later Kumâra Gupta of Magadha. The title is also found on the Bull coins recently discovered by Mr. Rivett-Carnac (Pl. III. 12).

The three Lion types (Lion-Trampler, Combatant Lion, and Retreating Lion) of Chandra Gupta II. may be regarded as imitations of the Tiger type of Samudra Gupta, and bear a reverse legend in the same form; the words *siṅha vikrama*, 'with the strength of a lion,' being substituted for *vyâghra parâkrama*, 'with the might of a tiger.'

In his Umbrella type of gold coins, Chandra Gupta II. uses the formula *Vikramâditya kshitim avajitya sucharati*, 'Vikramâditya having conquered the earth prospers,' and

[1] Corpus. Inscr. Ind. vol. iii. p. 27, note 4.

the same formula, with the substitution of the synonym *gâm* for *kshitim*, is used by Kumâra Gupta in his Swordsman type.

The special personal title of Kumâra Gupta was *Mahendra*, which has not been found on the coins of any other member of the dynasty. It occurs uncompounded only on Kumâra's gold coins. He uses it in combination with the participle *ajita* 'unconquered,' in his Horseman types, with *Śrî* in his Archer type, with *Kumâra* in his Peacock type, and with *Siṅha* in his Lion types (Combatant Lion and Lion-Trampler). A coin of the Combatant Lion type adds the word *parâkrama*, which generally occurs on the coins of Samudra Gupta only. The fuller compounded form *Mahendrâditya* is found on the Winged Peacock and Trident silver coins of Kumâra Gupta.

A Horseman to Left coin in the Bodleian cabinet gives Kumâra the title *Kramâjita*, 'of unconquered power,' which has not been found elsewhere, and his unique Two Queens coin presents the title *Śrî Pratâpa*.

The epithet *parama bhâgavata*, 'most devout worshipper of the holy one,' *scilicet* Vishṇu, is first met with on the coins of Chandra Gupta II., who uses it on his Vikramâditya silver coins, and his Horseman to Right and Horseman to Left gold pieces. The same epithet is used on the Winged Peacock silver coins of Kumâra Gupta and Skanda Gupta, and on the Bull silver coins of the latter prince.

The formula *vijitâvanir avanipati*, 'lord of the earth, who has conquered the earth,' is found on the Fantail Peacock coins of Kumâra Gupta, Skanda Gupta, Budha Gupta, Toramâṇa, Bhîma Sena, and Îśâna Varman, and is said by Thomas to occur on an unpublished gold Archer coin of Kumâra Gupta in the Freeling collection.

The legends of the Horseman (Right and Left) gold coins of Kumâra are unfortunately imperfect, but they seem to give him the title of *kshitipati*, a synonym of *avanipati*, 'lord of the earth.'

I read the title of *mahâkshatrapa* 'great Satrap' on a silver coin of Skanda Gupta in the British Museum, and believe the reading to be correct, but it requires confirmation.

The obverse legend of two Lion-Trampler gold coins of Kumâra Gupta clearly appears to include the words *Śrî Siksha* (or *Saiksha*) *devata*, but I cannot interpret them.

Nara, a successor of the Guptas in their Eastern dominions, took the title of *Bâlâditya*, 'the young' or 'rising sun.' The proper personal name of the king who assumed the title of *Prakâśâditya*, 'sun of splendour,' has not yet been deciphered.

CHAPTER V.—WEIGHTS.

Since the publication of my essay on the Gupta gold coins in 1884 I have seen a large number of coins not previously known to me, and have learned the weights of many, but the statistics collected five years ago remain still substantially correct. It seems, therefore, unnecessary to repeat in detail all the arguments then used to establish my positions. I shall content myself with a brief recapitulation of what is already on record, and with noting the few new facts available, and the modifications in my views which they suggest. Most of the Gupta gold coins follow the Indo-Scythian standard, which was apparently adopted from the Romans. We know from Pliny, whose Natural History was published in or about A.D. 77, that a great stream of Roman gold poured into India in his time, and the numerous finds of Roman coins in India prove that it continued for long after.

The *aureus* of Julius Cæsar in the specimens now existing ranges in weight from 120 to 125 grains. His standard is supposed to have been 125·66 grains. He was murdered B.C. 44. After his death the weight of the Roman *aureus* gradually declined, and is said to have averaged 115·39 grains in the reign of Nero (A.D. 54-68). Professor Gardner gives 114 grains as the highest known weight of Nero's *aurei*. The average weight of the *aurei* of Augustus in the British Museum is 121·26 grains.

The reasonings in my previous publication were based on the weighment of 177 gold Gupta coins. Subsequent discoveries do not materially alter the facts, and I therefore allow the figures to stand as before, with few exceptions. The highest weights are as follows :—

Reign.	*Type.*	*Grains.*
Chandra Gupta I.	King and Queen	123·8
Samudra Gupta	All	123·4
Kâcha (?=Samudra Gupta)	Standard	125·8
Chandra Gupta II.	Archer, wheel variety	132·5
,, ,,	Horseman to Right	130·92
,, ,,	Archer, common variety	127·6
,, ,,	Others	124·0
Kumâra Gupta	All	128·6
Skanda Gupta	Archer	132·5
Heavy coins of Chandra, etc.	All	148·7

I think that I formerly attached too much importance to average or mean weights. The really significant weighments are those of the best-preserved specimens, and I now confine my consideration to these.

My published table of weights gives as the highest weight of the Horseman to Right (Lancer) coins of Chandra Gupta II. 119·7 grains. A subsequently discovered coin of this type weighs 130·92 grains, and is thus made to conform in standard to the comparatively heavy Wheel variety of the Archer type of the same king, the heaviest specimen of which weighs 132·5 grains. I formerly supposed that the Horseman to Right (Lancer) coins were referable to a standard of 125, and the Wheel coins to a standard of 136·4 grains. Now it would seem as if this distinction were not sustainable, and I suspect that in my former paper I made too little allowance for wear and tear. The coins of Kumâra Gupta weigh, on the average, higher than those of his predecessors, but the top weight of any one coin of Kumâra Gupta's is only 128·6. Skanda Gupta's heaviest coin of the Archer type (not Kramâditya) weighs 132·5 grains, the same as the heaviest of the Wheel coins of Chandra Gupta II. I am inclined now to regard all these coins as struck according to a single standard, which seems to have been that of the Attic stater of 134·4 grains, transmitted through Roman, or possibly Syrian, channels.

I adhere to the opinion that the best-established value for the *rati*, the fundamental weight of the Indian scale, is 1·823 grain, which, for convenience, may be read as 1·825 grain, and that, consequently, the weight of the *suvarṇa* gold coin of 80 *ratis* ought to be 146 grains.

I think there can be no doubt that the heavy coins bearing the names of Chandra, Kumâra, Skanda Kramâditya, Nara Bâlâditya, and Prakâśâditya were intended to be of a standard different from that of the ordinary Gupta gold coins. The mean weight of these heavy coins is always, roughly speaking, about 20 grains greater than that of the regular Gupta coinage, and it is impossible that so great and constant a difference can be accidental.

The British Museum contains eleven pieces in base metal which bear the name of Kumâra, or its initial syllable, and the heaviest of these coins weighs as much as 151 grains. No safe conclusion as to weight standards can be drawn from coins of utterly base metal, and these debased coins of Kumâra must be excluded from consideration. They are certainly of later date than the death of Skanda Gupta, and probably belong to the later Kumâra Gupta of Magadha (*circa* A.D. 550), but no information as to their find-spots is available, and I cannot feel any certainty respecting their attribution.

The heavy coins of Chandra, which have been placed in the scales, weigh 144·5 and 148 grains, and bear the title Vikramâditya. The metal in these pieces does not apparently differ from the much-alloyed gold of many of the ordinary Archer coins of Chandra Gupta II., which ordinarily weigh about 123 grains. I know of no Chandra except Chandra Gupta II., to whom these heavy coins can be referred, and am now inclined to the opinion that they were struck during his reign, and formed a provincial coinage, probably issued from an Eastern mint.

The heavy Kumâra coins of tolerably good gold, four specimens of which are in the British Museum, weigh up to 148·7 grains. I cannot be certain whether they are a provincial issue of Kumâra Gupta of the Early Gupta dynasty, or were issued by the later Kumâra Gupta of Magadha.

I know of no Skanda except the Early Gupta king, and now believe that the heavy gold coins of Skanda with the title Kramâditya were issued by Skanda Gupta of the Early Gupta dynasty. The metal seems to be of much the same quality as that of his undoubted coins. The heavy coins of Skanda Kramâditya which have been weighed weigh from 141·4 to 146 grains.

The coins of Nara Bâlâditya and Prakâśâditya are certainly later than the time of Skanda Gupta, and were not issued by members of the Early Gupta dynasty. Many of the coins of Nara are of base metal. The heaviest of tolerably good gold weighs 146·5 grains. The heaviest Prakâśâditya coin weighs 146 2 grains.

It is, as I have said, useless to attempt to argue about the weights of coins struck in utterly base metal, but the heavy coins of Skanda Kramâditya, and some of those bearing the names of Chandra, Kumâra, Nara Bâlâditya, and Prakâśâditya are not obviously inferior in quality of metal to the undoubted coins of Chandra Gupta II., and it seems incredible that it should have been intended that these heavy coins, averaging about 144 grains, should have been struck, like the earlier Gupta coinage, to the standard of 134·4 grains. I still think that the intention was to adjust them to the Hindu *suvarṇa* standard of 146 grains. We cannot at present explain why this standard was adopted for some coins, and not for others, but I think it clear that both standards were in simultaneous use. The Gaṛhwâ (Gaḍhwâ) inscription from the Allâhâbâd District, which seems to have been recorded in the reign of Kumâra Gupta, especially mentions an endowment of nineteen *suvarṇas*, and the same inscription makes mention of *dînâras*. The name *suvarṇas* would properly be applied to the heavy class, and that of *dînâra* to the lighter class of Gupta coins. Unluckily this inscription is imperfect. (See *Corpus Inscr. Ind.* vol. iii. p. 264, No. 64.) Endowments of *dînâras* are mentioned in other Gupta inscriptions, *e.g.* in the Sânchi record dated 131 (*ibid*, p. 260, No. 62).

Specimens of the Gupta silver coins of Kumâra and Skanda

are so numerous that it would be absurd to give their weights in detail. The silver pieces of Chandra Gupta II., however, are extremely rare. The Freeling specimen of his Vikramânka type weighed 31 grains, and this is the only coin of his reign the weight of which I know. Specimens of the Winged Peacock type of Kumâra Gupta range in weight as high as 33 grains, or a fraction more, but average about 29. The Fantail Peacock coins of the same king are of about the same weight. Mr. Thomas observes that the weight of the Winged Peacock coins of Skanda Gupta "is more than ordinarily uneven, rising from 22½ to 33 grains." The highest weight noted for Skanda Gupta's Fantail Peacock coins is about 35 grains, and for his Bull type is 30 grains.

I am not able to give analyses of the metal in the silver coinage, but it is, like that of the gold coins, frequently impure. The figures given are, however, sufficient to show that all the Gupta silver coins were intended to be roughly equivalent to Attic hemidrachmæ, though they depart considerably from the standard weight.

The copper coins are rare, as compared with the silver, and it is possible to deal with their weights in more detail, but the coins are almost all in such bad condition that the investigation is not very profitable, and I cannot make out with certainty the standard according to which they were struck.

A much worn coin of the Umbrella type of Chandra Gupta II. weighs 102 grains, and another only 70·8. They may be intended for three-quarter *paṇa* pieces, of which the standard weight would be 109·5 grains.[1]

The Standing King coins range from 13·5 to 53·5 grains, and evidently include at least two denominations, but the specimens are all so worn, and the weights are so graduated, that I cannot say with confidence what the denominations were.

The British Museum specimens of the Vikramâditya Bust

[1] The *paṇa* in copper was the same weight as the *suvarṇa* in gold, and the equivalent in value of 80 cowrie shells, or a handful (*Arch. Rep.* vol. x. p. 78; vol. xiv. p. 17).

type weigh respectively 44 and 40·5 grains. Both these coins are in fair condition. I do not think the full weight can have exceeded 50 grains.

The Chandra Head coins are all small, and some are excessively minute. The lowest weight is 6·5 (or perhaps 4·5), and the highest 28 grains. I have sorted the coins into a larger size weighing from 16·5 to 28 grains, and a smaller size weighing from 6·5 (or perhaps 4·5) to 13 grains. I am inclined to think that three denominations of this type were issued, but the bad condition of the coins forbids any definite conclusions.

The little piece which weighs only 4·5 grains is very indistinct, and may belong to the Vase type of Chandra.

These curious little Vase coins occur in at least two sizes. A specimen of the larger kind weighs 13 grains, and the minute pieces range from 3½ to 7 grains. I do not think that these coins were issued by a member of the Gupta dynasty.

The metal of the Gupta copper coins seems to be of good quality.

Most of the gold coins are in weight *aurei* (=*didrachmæ*) of the standard of 134·4 grains, but some, as I have said, seem to have been struck to the Hindu standard of 146 grains. The genuine copper coinage, which was struck at Northern mints, is obviously related to the gold, and was doubtless intended to follow either the Græco-Roman or the Hindu standard, but I am unable to decide which was actually followed.

The minute copper coins of Skanda Gupta and Kumâra Gupta which follow the types of the silver coinage seem to be ancient forgeries.[1] They have been found in Kaṭhiâwâṛ.

Chapter VI.—Find-Spots and Mints.

In my former publication I gave minute details of the *provenance* of all the Gupta gold coins mentioned in my Catalogue, so far as known. It appears unnecessary to repeat

[1] See *post*, Chapter X. Supplement to Catalogue of Copper Coins, p. 144.

all those details, and I shall now confine myself to a general summary of the facts, adding details of the hoards of gold coins which have been discovered of late years, and a brief account of the *provenance* of the silver and copper coins.

The newly-discovered hoards of gold coins are as follows:

(1). The Tâṇḍâ hoard.

Tâṇḍâ is an old site in the Rai Barelî District of Oudh. The hoard was discovered in 1885, and consisted of twenty-five coins. Two of these belonged to the King and Queen type of Chandra Gupta I. The remaining twenty-three consisted of coins of Kâcha, and specimens of the Aśwamedha and Battle-axe types of Samudra Gupta, but, unfortunately, I omitted to note the exact numbers of each class. Specimens from this hoard are now in the Lucknow Museum, and seven coins belonging to it have been briefly noticed in print.[1]

(2). The Koṭwâ hoard.

This hoard was found at an ancient site named Koṭwâ in the Bânsgaon Tahsîl of the Gorakhpur District in the N.W.P., and a detailed description of it has been published by me.[2] Its contents were remarkably varied, as follows:—

Chandra Gupta II.	Archer type, class II., variety *a*, 5 specimens.
,, ,,	Lion-Trampler type, variety δ, 1 specimen.
Kumâra Gupta.	Archer type, class I., variety η, 1 specimen.
,, ,,	Horseman to Right type, variety *a*, 3 specimens.
,, ,,	Ditto, variety γ, 2 specimens.
,, ,,	Horseman to Left type, 1 specimen.
,, ,,	Peacock type, variety β, 2 specimens.
,, ,,	Lion-Trampler type, variety *a*, 1 specimen.

(3). The Bastî hoard.

This hoard was found, in August, 1887, at the site of an

[1] Proc. A.S.B. April, 1886, p. 68. Information respecting this hoard was first given me by Mr. E. Rose, of the P.W.D.

[2] Proc. A.S.B. July, 1887. I had not an opportunity of correcting the proofs of this paper, and regret that it is consequently disfigured by some misprints in the references.

old town in Mauza Sarai, close to the Jail of the civil station of Bastî, in the Bastî District of the N.W.P., which was then in my charge. Bastî is forty miles west of Gorakhpur, and lies between that town and Ajodhyâ. Eleven coins appear to have been found, but I only succeeded in purchasing ten for Government. Nine of these belong to the common variety of the Archer type (class II. *a*) of Chandra Gupta II. The tenth is a specimen of the rare Umbrella type of the same king. This coin is, I think, now in the Lucknow Museum.[1]

Mr. J. G. Sykes, Barrister-at-law, Lucknow, has favoured me with an inspection of nine Gupta gold coins in his cabinet, which were probably obtained in Oudh.

Mr. H. Rivett-Carnac has shown me sundry gold coins, obtained for the most part in or near Benares, which have passed through his hands, including fifteen specimens of the coinage of Skanda Kramâditya.

I understand that Mr. Hodges, of the P.W.D., has nineteen gold Gupta coins, all procured in Oudh, but I have not seen them.

I am indebted to Sir A. Cunningham for the following note on the find-spots of Gupta coins, which I give *verbatim*.

"The finds of gold Guptas are often concealed. Most of my coins have been obtained at the great places of pilgrimage, Mathurâ, Benares, and Gayâ. The silver Gupta coins[2] are chiefly found at Benares and country round about it, Ajudhya and country round about it, Mathurâ, and places in the neighbourhood. A fair number of silver Guptas have been obtained round about Sahâranpur and Bûriya on the Jumna.[3] The only records that I can find in my existing note-books are the following.[4]

[1] Proc. A.S.B. for 1887, p. 221.

[2] *Scilicet* those with reverse device of peacock with expanded tail, which I call Fantail Peacock coins.

[3] Haridwâr (Hurdwar), a famous place of pilgrimage, is in the Sahâranpur District of the North-Western Provinces.

[4] The rest of Sir A. Cunningham's valuable note-books were destroyed by the shipwreck of the P. and O. steamer Indus.

Gold.

At Gayâ:

1 Chandra Gupta I. (Chandra and Kumâra Devî).
1 Samudra (Parâkrama).
3 Chandra Gupta II. (S'rî Vikrama).
1 ,, ,, (Singha Vikrama).
1 Kumâra Gupta (Horseman).
1 Skanda Gupta (Kramâditya, single figure).

—

Total, 8.

At village near Kosam (in Allâhâbâd District):
1 Kumâra Gupta (Horseman).

At Soron on the Ganges (in the Etâ District, N.W.P.):
1 Chandra Gupta II. (S'rî Vikrama).

At Lucknow:
1 Samudra Gupta (Aśwamedha).

At Delhi:
1 Kumâra Gupta (Horseman).

—

Total, 12 gold Guptas in one year.

	SILVER.			COPPER.	
PLACE.	CHANDRA.	KUMÂRA.	SKANDA.	CHANDRA.	KUMÂRA.
Mathurâ	......	2	6	......	......
Ajudhya	......	......	......	10	......
Sankisa	......	......	1	......	......
Sultânganj on Ganges	1	......	......	......	......
Kosam	......	......	......	1	......
Ahichhatra...	......	......	......	2	1
Sunit, close to Ludiâna	......	......	......	1	......
TOTAL	1	2	7	14	1
	TOTAL... 10			TOTAL 15	

"I have seen a large number of silver Guptas, but latterly have refused all without dates.

"The northern silver coins with the peacock with spread tail are tolerably common. The western silver coins of Kumâra with standing peacock are very common in Gujarât.

"I have a considerable number of silver Guptas, and a fair collection of copper Guptas, but the copper are confined to Chandra, with the single exception of one Kumâra. I formerly possessed a better copper coin of Kumâra, which Tregear got from Ajodhya. I think it may now be in the Bodleian Library at Oxford."[1]

The hoards noticed in my essay on the gold coins were those found at

1. Jaichandra's Mahal, Jaunpur, by Mr. Tregear. A small number of coins of various reigns;—

2. Bharsar, near Benares. About 160 coins of the reigns of Samudra Gupta, Chandra Gupta II., Kumâra Gupta, Skanda Gupta, and Prakâśâditya. 71 pieces are known to have belonged to the reign of Chandra Gupta II.;—

3. At Muhammadpur, in Jessore District, Bengal. Gold and silver Gupta coins of various reigns, mixed with coins of later date, including one of Śaśângka, A.D. 600;—

4. At Gopâlpur, in the Gorakhpur District, Bengal. 20 gold coins, of which seven belonged to the reign of Chandra Gupta II.;—

5. At Allâhâbâd. About 200 pieces of the Peacock type of Kumâra Gupta;—

6. At Jhûsî, opposite Allâhâbâd. 20 or 30 gold coins of Kumâra Gupta;—

7. At Hûglî. 13 gold coins of Samudra Gupta, Chandra Gupta II., and Kumâra Gupta;—

8. On the border between the Gonda District, Oudh, and the Bastî District, N.W.P. The exact number of coins is not known, but several of Mr. Hooper's specimens are from this find. This hoard was not explicitly mentioned in my former essay, though alluded to in the notes on Mr. Hooper's coins.

[1] Letter dated 27th January, 1888. Sankisa is in the Farrukhâbâd District, N.W.P.; Sultânganj is in the Bhâgalpur District, Bengal; Kosam is in the Allâhâbâd District, N.W.P.; Ahichhatra (Râmnagar) is in the Barelî District, N.W.P.; and Sunit is in the Lûdiâna District, Panjâb. The copper coin of Kumâra, collected by Tregear, is in the Bodleian cabinet.

The statistics previously published by me proved that the total of indisputably gold coins found east of Kanauj was then known to be about 480, only five or six being known to have been obtained at Kanauj, and 10 to the west or north-west of that city. I therefore observed that "the evidence now presented fully warrants the assertion that the find-spots of the Gupta gold coins in no way support the statement that Kanauj was the Gupta capital." The fresh evidence amply confirms this proposition. Two of the newly-discovered hoards, those of Koṭwâ and Bastî, were found in the districts of the N.W.P. east of Oudh, and the third, that of Tâṇḍâ, was found in the province of Oudh, which is to the east of Kanauj.[1] A few stray specimens of Gupta gold coins have been picked up in the western districts, or even in the Panjâb, but very few, except at certain places of pilgrimage, and the fact is certain that the study of the gold coinage indicates no special connection of the Gupta dynasty with Kanauj, and there is not the slightest reason to suppose that the Gupta gold coins were minted at that city.

The evidence as to the find-spots of the silver and copper coins supports the same negative proposition.

The principal locality from which the copper coins are obtained is the ancient Hindu city of Ajodhyâ (Ayudhyâ), near Faizâbâd on the banks of the Ghâgra on the eastern border of Oudh. Ten out of fifteen specimens of the copper coinage in Sir A. Cunningham's cabinet were obtained at this place, from which Tregear also procured his unique specimen of the Standing King type of Kumâra Gupta. The five copper coins in Mr. Hooper's cabinet were all collected at Ajodhya.

Ahichhatra (Râmnagar), in the Barelî District of the North-Western Provinces, far to the north-west, has yielded two copper coins of Chandra Gupta, and one, which is doubtfully ascribed to Kumâra Gupta. Two copper pieces of

[1] Kanauj is in the Farrukhâbâd or Fatehgaṛh District of the North-Western Provinces. An account of its history and a description of the few remains now existing on its site will be found in Cunningham's Arch. Rep. vol. i. pp. 279 *seqq*.

Chandra Gupta have been obtained in the Panjâb, namely, one by Mr. Theobald at Pânîpat, near Delhi, and the other by Sir A. Cunningham at Sunit, near Lûdiâna. One has been procured at Kosam in the Allâhâbâd District.

It is quite clear that the copper coinage, like the gold, has no special connection with Kanauj. The copper coins of Chandra Gupta II. are not so rare as has sometimes been supposed. I know that many specimens exist in the cabinets of the Asiatic Society of Bengal, the Lucknow Museum, and private collectors, respecting which I have not been able to procure details. My catalogue notices in detail more than fifty pieces, and I should say that at least as many more exist scattered in various collections. It is unfortunate that more copious information respecting the find-spots of the copper coins is not available, because copper coins are rarely dug up far from their place of mintage, and, if we knew the find-spots of the copper coins with accuracy, we should know the position of the Gupta copper mints.

The negative proposition, that the copper coinage had no special connection with Kanauj, having been established, I think that the fact of sixteen Gupta copper coins having been obtained (and presumably found) at the ancient city of Ajodhya fully warrants the positive inference that a mint for copper coinage was maintained, certainly by Chandra Gupta II., and probably by Kumâra Gupta, at that place. The remaining evidence concerning the *provenance* of the Gupta copper is too imperfect to justify any further positive conclusions, but it is not improbable that Ahichhatra also was a mint-city.

The Gupta copper coins are sometimes found associated with those of the Mitra (Sunga) dynasty, which are obtained in considerable numbers at Ajodhya and in the neighbourhood.

The silver Gupta coinage was provincial. It is, in all its forms, beyond doubt a continuation of the Satrap coinage of Saurâshtra, which was imitated from Græco-Bactrian hemidrachmæ, and it it can hardly be doubted that the form of the Satrap coinage was first adopted by Chandra Gupta II. when he conquered Saurâshtra and Guzerat. The Udayagiri inscription shows that he was in Mâlwâ in the year 82 G.E., equivalent to A.D. 401–402,[1] but the precise date of the western conquests is not known. Kumâra Gupta and Skanda Gupta retained possession of these conquests, and issued large quantities of silver coinage, and, after the death of Skanda Gupta, his successor in the west, Budha Gupta, and likewise Toramâṇa and Bhîma Sena, who succeeded Budha Gupta, continued to strike silver coins of the same general pattern.[2]

As I have said, all the Gupta silver coins are intended to be roughly equivalent in weight to hemidrachmæ, and all are clearly derived from the Satrap coins of Saurâshtra, the obverse device of which is continued throughout the series without material change. But the reverse devices of the Gupta silver coins divide the coinage into at least three distinct classes, which may be called the Winged Peacock, the Bull, and the Fantail Peacock. The main reverse device on the very rare silver coins of Chandra Gupta II. is a rude representation of a bird (presumably a peacock, but possibly intended for Garuḍa) standing to front with wings expanded but the tail concealed. Excepting one specimen, which was found at Sultânganj in the Bhâgalpur District, Bengal,[3] associated with a coin of Swâmî Rudra Siṅha, the last Satrap of Saurâshtra,[4] all the silver coins of Chandra Gupta II. appear to have been found in Kaṭhiâwâṛ or Guzerat. I have no doubt that they were struck at some place or places in either of those provinces.

Kumâra Gupta struck immense quantities of silver coins with the same reverse device, some bearing the title of Râjâdhirâjâ, and some the higher title of Mahârâjâdhirâjâ. I believe specimens of these coins are occasionally found in Northern India, but all of which I know particulars were found in the same provinces as the coins of Chandra Gupta II., and were certainly struck at mints there situated.

[1] Cunningham, Arch. Rep. vol. x. pp. 49, 51; Corpus Inscr. Ind vol. iii.

[2] Cunningham, Arch. Rep. vol. ix. p. 26. The unique coin of Bhîma Sena has been presented by Mr. H. Rivett-Carnac to the British Museum, which also possesses the only two known specimens of Toramâṇa's coinage.

[3] Now in the Indian Imperial Museum, Calcutta.

[4] Cunningham, Arch. Rep. vol. x. p. 127.

Skanda Gupta struck coins bearing the title Kramâditya, some of which have the reverse device the same as on the coins of Chandra Gupta II. and of Kumâra Gupta, while the majority bear a rude device which seems to be a modified form of it, but which has generally been described as an 'altar.' His silver coins bearing the title Vikramâditya all have the degraded altar-like device. All these varieties of Skanda Gupta's silver coinage seem to have been issued from Western mints.

A few coins of Skanda Gupta have as reverse device a recumbent bull, associated with the title Kramâditya. I have no precise information as to the find-spots of these coins, but, considering that the recumbent bull was the cognizance of the Kings of Valabhi in Saurâshtra, I presume that they were struck in the Western provinces.

The third leading reverse device of the Gupta silver coinage is that of the standing peacock, with tail fully expanded. Coins of this type were struck by Kumâra Gupta and Skanda Gupta of the Imperial dynasty, by Budha Gupta, by Toramâṇa, who seems to have succeeded him in Mâlwâ, by Bhîma Sena, of whom a single coin has been obtained at Ajodhya, and by Îśâna Varman of Magadha.

The single trident coin of Kumâra, described by Mr. Newton, was also a Western coin. It is perhaps possible to regard its device as a modification of the winged bird, but in the drawing it seems to be a trident, and nothing else; and, if the drawing is correct, we must admit the existence of a fourth trident class of silver coins.

The only known inscription of Budha Gupta is at Eraṇ in Mâlwâ dated 165 G.E., and it indicates that he ruled the country between the Jumna and the Narbadâ,[1] but the few known examples of his coinage have been obtained at or near Benares, and are dated 174. It is impossible to say where they were struck. Toramâṇa, like Budha, ruled in Mâlwâ. Only two specimens of his coinage are known to me. They are both in the British Museum, one being part of the Bush

[1] Cunningham, Arch. Rep. vol. x. p. 81; Corpus Inscr. Ind. vol. iii. p. 88, No. 19.

collection, and one presented by Miss Baring. Both bear the date 52, of which the interpretation is doubtful.[1]

As in the case of Budha Gupta, it is impossible to say where Toramâṇa's coins were struck.

The Fantail Peacock coins of Kumâra Gupta and Skanda Gupta were certainly struck chiefly, if not altogether, at mints in the Northern Provinces. I have already quoted Sir A. Cunningham's testimony that they are chiefly found at or near Benares, Ajodhya, Mathurâ, and Sahâranpur, all of which places are situated in the North-Western Provinces. A few have been obtained at Kanauj. The coins of both reigns are tolerably common, but I think those of Skanda Gupta are scarcer than those of his predecessor. I am not aware of any evidence that indicates the precise position of the mints from which the Northern silver coinage issued. The principal mint was presumably at the capital.

The Western silver coinage appears to have been a purely provincial issue, and was probably struck at the capital of Saurâshtra, which was very likely Jûnâgarh, close to which the great inscription of Skanda Gupta's reign is incised on the Girnâr rock.

The evidence clearly proves that the gold and copper coins were struck and chiefly current in territories far to the east of Kanauj, which territories may be roughly described as the Province of Benares, with some adjoining districts. The distribution of the architectural and sculptural remains of the Gupta dynasty confirms the testimony of the coins, and distinctly indicates that the capital of the Northern dominions of the Gupta Kings lay either between Allâhâbâd (Prayâg) on the west, and Patna (Pâṭaliputra) on the east, or at one of those cities. This is the region indicated by the Purâṇas as the seat of their power, and not the Doâb, or country between the Ganges and Jumna in which Kanauj is situated.

The Vâyu Purâṇa states that Sâketa was included in their

[1] Sir A. Cunningham reads the date of one as 53, but I agree with Mr. Fleet in reading the dates on both specimens as 52. The character = which stands for 2 is a little blurred on one coin. Mr. Fleet reads the date on Budha Gupta's coins as 175, but Sir A. Cunningham's reading of 174 is supported by the evidence of an inscription dated in words and figures.

dominions, and there can be no doubt that it was, whether we identify that city with Ajodhya, as Sir A. Cunningham proposes, or with Lucknow as suggested by Mr. Fergusson.[1]

The first two princes of the dynasty, Gupta and Ghaṭotkacha, assumed only the subordinate title of Mahârâjâ, and seem to have been mere feudatory chiefs, presumably subject to an Indo-Scythian sovereign. It is improbable that they coined money, and they have left no inscriptions, and consequently we know nothing about them, except that they were respectively grandfather and father of Chandra Gupta I., the first independent sovereign of the dynasty. Probably their principality was in the neighbourhood of Pâṭaliputra. Chandra Gupta I. married Kumâra Devî of the Lichchhavi family of Nepâl, and the prominent record of this fact, both on coins and in inscriptions, is good evidence that the alliance was important. It may reasonably be assumed that it helped Chandra Gupta I. in his rise to greatness. I formerly supposed that the Lichchhavi family into which he married was that of Vaisâli near Pâṭaliputra, but recent discoveries show that the alliance was with the ruling family of Nepâl, of which the Vaisâli Lichchhavis were probably a branch.[2]

Mr. Hooper has suggested to me that Ajodhya may have been the Gupta capital. I have shown that there is reason to believe that it was the seat of a copper mint in the reigns of Chandra Gupta II. and Kumâra Gupta, and, from the reign of Chandra Gupta I., it must have been one of the chief cities of the dynasty. Sir A. Cunningham has collected at Ajodhya traditions of kings named Samudra Pâla and Chandra Pâla, which seem to be confused reminiscences of the great Gupta dynasty.[3]

[1] Cunningham, Arch. Rep. vol. i. p. 317. Fergusson, Archæology in India (Trübner, London, 1884), pp. 110—115. Mr. Fergusson's suggestion that excavations should be made in the numerous mounds which exist in Lucknow deserves attention. I am inclined to think that he was right in identifying Lucknow with Sâketa.

[2] *See* Hewitt on Early History of Northern India in J.R.A.S. Vol. XX. N.S p. 356. The Vajjian or Vṛijjian confederacy included nine tribes of Lichchhavis and nine tribes of Mallis. Mr. Hewitt thinks that these tribes were of Kolarian race. Some ill-supported speculations of Mr. Beal on the subject will be found in J.R.A.S. Vol. XIV. N.S. p. 39.

[3] Arch. Rep. vol. xi. p. 99. The forged Gayâ inscription of Samudra Gupta purports to have been executed at Ajodhya, and issued from the camp of Samudra

But, I am still of opinion that Pâṭaliputra has the best claim to be considered the Gupta capital. In the fourteenth line of the Allâhâbâd Pillar inscription, which was recorded early in the reign of Chandra Gupta II. (*i.e. circa* A.D. 390 to 400), the city of Pushpapura is spoken of in connection with Samudra Gupta in such a way as to indicate that it was his capital. Mr. Fleet is inclined to think that the name Pushpapura is intended to mean Kusumapura, which was a name of Kanauj.[1] It is true that in Sanskrit Kusumapura and Pushpapura have the same meaning, 'flower-city,' but it seems to me that when we know that the former synonym was appropriated to Kanauj, and the latter to Pâṭaliputra,[2] we are not warranted in making the gratuitous assumption that the names were exchanged in the Allâhâbâd inscription. I repeat that there is not a tittle of evidence of any kind that Kanauj was the Gupta capital, and there is not the slightest reason for scepticism as to the testimony of the Allâhâbâd inscription that Pushpapura or Pâṭaliputra was the capital of Samudra Gupta. Its evidence is confirmed by the references to Pâṭaliputra under that name in two records of Chandra Gupta II.

The Guptas had no more to do with Kanauj than they had to do with Mathurâ or Gayâ, or any other big city in their empire; but errors die hard, and I suppose that, because Prinsep used an incautious phrase fifty years ago, people will still, fifty years hence, insist on speaking of 'the Guptas of Kanauj.'

There is no reason to suppose that either Lower Bengal or the Panjâb was included in the Gupta empire. Its eastern boundary was probably in the neighbourhood of Bhâgalpur, and its western near Delhi. During the reigns of Chandra Gupta II., Kumâra Gupta, and Skanda (*circa* A.D. 390 to 480) it included the territories which are now known as Bihâr (North and South), the North-west Provinces and Oudh, Central India, Guzerât, and Kâṭhiâwâṛ.

Gupta there. This shows that at the begining of the eighth century A.D. Ajodhya was believed to have been one of the chief cities of Samudra Gupta.

[1] Corpus Inscr. Ind. vol. iii. p. 5.

[2] *Eg.* in the Nepâl inscription of Jaya Deva dated Samvat 153 (*scilicet* of S'rî Harsha era = A.D. 759–60), published in *Ind. Ant.* vol. ix. p. 180.

Chapter VII.—Authorities.

The public collections of coins to which I have had access are the following:

(1) Asiatic Society of Bengal (A.S.B.).[1]
(2) Bodleian (B.).[2]
(3) British Museum (B.M.).
(4) India Office (I.O.).[3]
(5) Royal Asiatic Society (R.A.S.).[4]

The private collectors who have been good enough to favour me with inspection of their coins are:

(1) Major-Gen. Sir Alexander Cunningham, K.C.I.E., etc. (A.C.).[5]
(2) Alexander Grant, Esq., C.I.E. (A.G.).
(3) H. Rivett-Carnac, Esq., C.I.E., Bengal Civil Service (C.).
(4) The late Sir E. C. Bayley, K.C.S.I. (E.C.B.).
(5) John Hooper, Esq., Bengal Civil Service (H.).
(6) J. G. Sykes, Esq., Barrister-at-law, Lucknow (S.).
(7) W. Theobald, Esq. (W.T.).

The known hoards of gold coins have been enumerated in Chapter VI.

I have no doubt that large numbers of Gupta coins exist in private cabinets which I have not seen, and it is quite possible that they may include some unpublished types. I hope the possessors will look up their specimens, and endeavour to fill up the gaps in my exposition of the subject.

The publication of this monograph will, I trust, in general render superfluous reference to earlier publications, but the appended bibliographical list may be of some use.

[1] I have not seen the cabinet of the Asiatic Society of Bengal, and am dependent for my knowledge of it on rough notes supplied by Dr. Hoernlé, and a few published notices of individual coins.

[2] See the detailed catalogue *post* p. 61.

[3] The India Office collection has been presented by the Secretary of State for India to the British Museum. Mr. E. J. Rapson has given me much assistance in examining the coins under his care.

[4] The Royal Asiatic Society collection contains no coins of value.

[5] I am specially indebted to Sir A. Cunningham for the liberality with which he placed his knowledge and cabinet at my disposal.

Gold Coinage.

1. Col. Tod's paper in Trans. Roy. As. Soc. (1827), Vol. I. p. 340, and pl. xii. 4th series. 4 coins, figures 1–4.

2. H. H. Wilson's paper in Asiatic Researches, vol. xvii. and pl. i. figures 5, 7, 12, 13, 17, 18, 19.

3. Marsden's Numismata Orientalia, Nos. ml.–mlix. inclusive.

4. Wilson's Ariana Antiqua, pl. xviii. figures 1–14 and 16–28.

5. E. Thomas's Revised Catalogue of Gupta gold coins in his edition of Prinsep's Essays, (1858), vol. i. pp. 377–387. Thomas's original catalogue of gold coins was published in J.A.S.B. vol. xxiv. (1855), pp. 487–502.

The plates of gold coins in Thomas's edition reproduce J. Prinsep's plates in the J.A.S.B. as follows:—

P.E.	Pl.	xxii.	figs.	16 and 17 =	J.A.S.B.	vol. iv.	pl.	xxxviii.
,,	,,	xxiii.	,,	18 to 32 =	,,	,,	,,	xxxix.
,,	,,	xxix.	,,	11 to 20 =	,,	,, v.	,,	xxxvi.
,,	,,	xxx.	,,	1 to 10 =	,,	,,	,,	xxxviii.

J. Prinsep's plates are also reproduced in J.R.A.S. Vol. XII. (o.s.), 1850, and two of them (pl. xxii. and xxix. of P.E.) were reprinted by Mr. H. T. Prinsep as plates x. and xi. of his Note on the Historical Discoveries deducible from the Recent Discoveries in Afghanistan (London, 1844). A portion of J. Prinsep's plates is badly copied in the plate facing page 28 of the late Mr. Wilton Oldham's Historical and Statistical Memoir of the Ghaziepoor District.

6. E. Thomas's Records of the Gupta Dynasty (Trübner, 1876), pp. 21–24, and Autotype plate, figures 1–5. This work is a reprint of chapter iii. in vol. ii. of the Reports of the Archæological Survey for Western India (1874–75), compiled by Mr. James Burgess.

7. Kittoe and Bayley, Memo. on Ancient Gold Coins found at Bharsar, near Benares, in J.A.S.B. vol. xxi. (1852), pp. 390–400, and plate xii. figures 1–9.

8. Sundry minor notices, chiefly in the Proceedings of the Asiatic Society of Bengal.

9. Classified and Detailed Catalogue by V. A. Smith, in J.A.S.B. vol. liii. (1884), part i. p. 119, with 5 plates.

10. Indian Antiquary, for March and June, 1885, vol. xiv.

11. W. Theobald, On certain Symbols or Devices on the Gold Coins of the Guptas, J.A.S.B. vol. liv. part i. p. 84.

SILVER COINAGE.

1. E. Thomas in P.E. vol. ii. pp. 94–101, plate xxxvii. figs. 16, 17, for coins other than the Fantail Peacock types, and P.E. vol. i. p. 338, pl. xxvii. 10–12 for the latter; also P.E. vol. i. pl. iv. 20.

The corresponding original notes and plates of J. Prinsep are:—

J.A.S.B. vol. iii. p. 230, pl. xviii. fig. 20=P.E. vol. i. pl. iv. fig. 20.

J.A.S.B. vol. iv. p. 687, pl. xlix. figs. 10, 11, 12,=P.E. vol. i. p. 338, pl. xxvii. figs. 10–12.

J.A.S.B. vol. v. pl. xii.=P.E. ii. pl. xxxvii. figs. 16, 17.

2. E. Thomas, J.A.S.B. vol. xxiv. pp. 503–518.

3. E. Thomas, J.A.S.B. vol. xxvii. p. 255.

4. E. Thomas, J.R.A.S. Vol. XIII. (N.S.) p. 548, and J.R.A.S. Vol. XII. (O.S.) p. 65, pl. ii. figs. 39–53.

5. E. Thomas, Records of Gupta Dynasty, pp. 44–55, and autotype plate, from fig. 6.

6. Newton, in J.Bo.R.A.S. vol. vii. (1862), pp. 3, 10, and plate, and *ibid.* vol. ix. p. 1 (1868.)

7. Ariana Antiqua, pl. xv. 17, 18, 20.

8. Cunningham, Arch. Rep. vol. ix. p. 23, pl. v.

9. Fleet, in Indian Antiquary, March, 1885, vol. xiv. p. 65; and E. C. Bayley, *ibid.* vol. vi. p. 57.

10. Sundry minor notices.

COPPER COINAGE.

P.E. vol. i. pp. 374–375, pl. xxx. figures 11–15, corresponding to J.A.S.B. vol. iv. pl. xxxviii.

A.A. pl. xxviii. fig. 15.

J.A.S.B. vol. xxxiv. (1865), p. 125, and pl. v. figures 20 and 21.

J.A.S.B. vol. liii. (1884), p. 121, *note.*

The British Museum and India Office collections of gold coins were examined by me in 1883. I have now carefully re-examined all the gold coins in both cabinets, correcting the errors in my previous observations, and have also scrutinized every specimen of the copper and silver coinage in the same collections. When my essay on the gold coins was published, I was dependent for information concerning the coins in the Bodleian Library on imperfect notes supplied by the late Mr.

W. S. W. Vaux, F.R.S. I have now had an opportunity of personally examining the coins, and am in a position to give a detailed account of them.

The cabinet of the Bodleian Library at Oxford contains a large number, though not at all a complete series, of Gupta coins.

The Gupta and other Hindu coins in this cabinet have never been carefully catalogued, and were, at the time of my examination of them, very erroneously arranged and labelled. Numismatists will, therefore, I presume, be glad to be supplied with an accurate list of the Bodleian Gupta coins.

When inspecting the collection, I had not leisure to thoroughly examine the silver coins, but, so far as I perceived, they include no novelty. A few silver pieces are labelled as belonging to certain of the so-called Sâh Kings (the Satraps of Saurâshṭra). Fifteen specimens are labelled as 'Sâh uncertain,' and this batch includes the Gupta coins, which are all of the Fantail Peacock type. I identified three of these coins, namely, No. 785, Skanda Gupta, No. 789, Budha Gupta, and one coin of Kumâra Gupta. Two of the coins bear the trident *(triśûl)* reverse device, and are probably coins of the Bhaṭârka princes of Valabhi, but I did not succeed in deciphering the legends. It is quite possible that, on close examination of the trays of unclassed coins, some other silver Guptas may be discovered.

All the Gupta coins appear to belong to the collection presented to the Bodleian Library by Mr. J. Bardoe Elliott in 1859, part of which was purchased by that gentleman from Mr. Tregear in 1848. Some of the specimens belonged at one time to Sir A. Cunningham.

I made a careful and minute examination of all the gold and copper coins. Two of the latter were picked out of a tray containing a most miscellaneous collection of unclassed coins. The following catalogue is correct, and will facilitate the accurate labelling of the gold and copper Gupta coins.

Catalogue of the Gold and Copper Gupta Coins in the Bodleian Library.

Gold.

Reign.	*Type and Variety.*	*No. of Label.*
Chandra Gupta I.	King and Queen	683
Samudra Gupta	Javelin, *a*	686, 686 *bis*, 687, 687 *bis*, 688–691, 692 (*on label* 892)
	Archer, *a*	693
	Aśwamedha, *a*	694, 695
	,, *β*	696
Kâcha (?=Samudra Gupta)	Standard	678, 679
Chandra Gupta II.	Archer, Class I., *a*	708
	,, Class I., *β*	709
	,, Class II., *a*	697–706
	Horseman to r.	732
	,, l., *a*	710, 711
	,, l., *β*	713
	Lion-Trampler, *a*	725
	,, *γ*	724
	,, *δ*	726
	Umbrella	680–682
Kumâra Gupta	Swordsman	717
	Archer, Class I.	714–716
	,, Class II.	719, 735, 736
	Horseman to r., *a*	712
	,, *β*	731
	,, *γ*	734
	,, l.	733
Skanda Kramâditya	Archer	684, 727, 728, 730
Nara Bâlâditya		718, 720–723, 729

Copper.

Chandra Gupta II.	Umbrella	752
	Standing King	750, 753, and one not numbered
	Chandra Head, large	754
	,, ,, small	one not numbered
Kumâra Gupta	Standing King	751

Abstract.

GOLD.

Chandra Gupta I., Samudra Gupta, Kâcha, Chandra Gupta II., Kumâra Gupta, and Skanda Kramâditya, 54 coins; Nara Bâlâditya, 6 coins.

COPPER.

Chandra Gupta II., 6 coins; Kumâra Gupta, 1 coin.

The coins bearing the following numbers, namely, 737, 738, 740, 740 *bis*, and 741–747, belong to the class of Indo-Scythian coins with Nâgarî legends, which have been described by Mr. Thomas.[1] Nos. 741 and 742 have the name Bhadra to the left of the spear, and resemble the coins described by me.[2]

Nos. 741–746 are like silver in colour, but were probably intended to pass as gold currency. No. 747 is of base pale gold. Nos. 738 and 740 are gold coins of the Bhṛi Shaka type.

A manuscript list, signed A. Cunningham, shows that the Tregear collection had contained 8 copper coins of Chandra Gupta II., viz. 3 'bust,' 2 'half-length,' and 3 'Mahârâjâ.' The last must have been of the Umbrella type. The total number of Gupta copper coins now in the Bodleian collection is seven.[3]

CHAPTER VIII.—CATALOGUE OF GOLD COINS.

CONTENTS.

[1] Indian Antiquary, vol. xii. Jan. 1883.

[2] J.A.S.B. vol. liii. part i. p. 172, plate iv. 6.

[3] I am indebted to Mr. E. B. Nicholson, the Bodleian Librarian, for the grant of special facilities for the examination of the four trays containing Gupta coins, and for perusal of a book of manuscript correspondence concerning the Elliott collection. The Bodleian coin cabinet has, unfortunately, been much neglected in the past, and, until it is properly arranged, its contents can be of little use to numismatists. The Muhammadan coins have recently been arranged by Mr. Stanley Lane Poole, whose catalogue has been published. The other Indian coins are, as yet, in confusion, and no dependence can be placed on such labelling as has been attempted. The Librarian intends, I understand, to proceed with the arrangement of the whole cabinet, and to take steps for making it more accessible to students than it used to be.

CHANDRA GUPTA I.

King and Queen Type.

Obv. King, wearing tailed-coat and close-fitting cap, standing to l. facing queen, who looks to r. King's r. hand raised, his l. arm resting on spear, surmounted by crescent.

Under king's l. arm च न्द्र | गु प्त 'Chandra Gupta.'

Behind queen कुमार देवी श्री : 'Kumâra Devî S'rî.'

Rev. Goddess, holding fillet in r. hand, and cornucopiæ in l. arm, seated on couchant lion, which faces either r. or l.

Legend in field near r. margin लिच्छवय:, '*Lichchhavayaḥ*, 'the Lichchhavis.' Mon.

References and Remarks.—Variety a. Rev. lion to r.

B.M. Purchased. Crescent between heads of king and queen. Condition good. Mon. 3*a*. Wt. 123·8. (Pl. I. Fig. 1.)

B.M. Marsden mlviii. Brought from India by Lord Valentia (Mountmorris). Mon. 5. Wt. 115·3.

B.M. Swiney. Mon. 4*b*. Wt. 118·2. Figured in A.A. pl. xviii. 3.

C. One specimen obtained at Ghâzîpur. Wt. 119. Another obtained at Benares. Wt. 119·5.

A.C. P.E. i. 369, pl. xxix. 15.

Stacy. Mon. 8*d*. A duplicate in Tregear cabinet.

Tâṇḍâ hoard. One specimen.

Variety β. Rev. lion to l.

B. Mon. 4*a*.

W.T. Mon. 22*b*. Wt. 113. Bought at Benares.

Tâṇḍâ hoard. One specimen.

S. Wt. 112·5. Obtained either at Lucknow or Fyzabad. Mon. apparently 8*a*. (Proc.A.S.B. pl. v. 4.)

Sir A. Cunningham has in his cabinet three examples of this type, one of which I have noted as belonging to variety *a*. One of his coins was procured at Gayâ, and another at Nîmkhâr or Nîmsâr, on the banks of the Gumtî, a very sacred site in the Sîtâpur District, Oudh.

The legend 'Lichchhavayaḥ' records the marriage of the king into the Lichchhavi family of Nepâl. The stone inscriptions mention this alliance, and also state the queen's name, as given on the coins.

Compare the rev. device with the sandstone sculpture, M. 10,

CHANDRA GUPTA I.—*continued.*

believed to be from Mathurâ, in the Indian Museum, Calcutta. "The figure is that of a woman, seated on the back of an undoubted lion. The left leg is bent at the knee, and the left knee rests on the head of the lion, the left foot being drawn up almost under the body in front, thus resting on the lion's back. The foot, however, as in the majority of Buddhist figures, has not the sole upturned. The right limb is only partially bent, and the foot rests on the side of the lion. . . . The most interesting feature of this sculpture, however, is the child, which is represented lying across the left thigh of the figure, resting on the left hand, the feet of the infant hanging down against the hind part of the left leg of the statuette." (*Anderson, Catalogue and Handbook of the Archæological Collections in the Indian Museum,* part i. p. 184.) Also compare the effigies of the Greek Cybele, and of the Syrian Great Goddess.

SAMUDRA GUPTA.

Tiger Type.

Obv. King standing to r., wearing tight Indian waist-cloth, turban, necklace, armlets, and large earrings, trampling on body of tiger, which is falling backwards, while he shoots it in the mouth. Bow in king's r. hand, his l. is raised above his shoulder.

Imperfect legend on r. margin व्याघ्र [पराक्रमः], *vyâghra* [*parâkrama*], 'with the might of a tiger.'

Rev. Goddess to l., standing on a monster facing l., which has an elephant's head, and scaly fish's tail. Her r. hand is extended across a standard or spear, tipped with a crescent, and adorned with pennons. An expanded lotus-flower in her l. hand.

Legend near margin to r. राजा समुद्र गुप्तः, *Râjâ Samudra Guptaḥ.* No mon.

References and Remarks.

B.M. **Eden.** At present unique. Wt. 116·6. Described and figured in Records, p. 21, fig. 2 of plate. (Pl. I. Fig. 2.)

The execution of this coin is good, and the design spirited. The reading *parâkrama* in the obv. legend is probable, but not certain, the character for *kra* only being legible. The

SAMUDRA GUPTA—*continued.*

crescent-tipped spear or standard is also found on the coins of Chandra Gupta I. and the Battle-axe coins of Samudra Gupta. The reverse goddess is probably intended to represent the consort of Varuṇa = Samudra, the ocean, or god of the waters, *ante*, p. 20. The standing figure of the goddess connects this type with the Aśwamedha type of Samudra Gupta and Kumâra Gupta, the Standard type of Kâcha, and the Umbrella type of Chandra Gupta II. The resemblance to the last-named type is especially close, because in one variety of it the goddess appears to stand likewise on a monster.

I place this Tiger type first in the list of the issues of Samudra Gupta on account of the simple title Râjâ assumed by the king. In his other coins he assumes more ambitious titles. The obverse device served as the model for the Lion types of Chandra Gupta II. and Kumâra Gupta.

Aśwamedha Type.

Obv. Horse, standing to l., unattended, and occupying most of field. In front of horse an altar, from which springs a bent pole, carrying three long streamers, which occupy top of field.

Between horse's legs the syllable सि, *Si*, sometimes standing on an altar or pedestal.

Marginal legend imperfect; it includes the title राजाधिराज *Râjâdhirâja*, followed by पृथिवीं जित्य or जयति, *prithivîm jitya* or *jayati*, a boast of having conquered the earth.

Rev. Female, standing to l., holding in r. hand handle of yak's tail fly-whisk (*chaurî*), which rests on her r. shoulder. Her left hand hangs empty by her side. In front of her a spear or standard adorned with pennons. Legend in r. field अश्वमेध पराक्रमः, *aśwamedha parâkramaḥ*, 'with power to perform the *aśwamedha* sacrifice.' No mon.

References and Remarks.—Variety a. Without pedestal under सि.

B.M. Eden. Wt. 117. (Pl. I. Fig. 4.)
B.M. Payne Knight. Wt. 113·2. Condition poor.

SAMUDRA GUPTA—*continued.*

B.M. Thomas. Wt. 117. Ditto. Seems to be the coin from Sahâranpur figured in A.A. pl. xviii. 2.

B.M. Prinsep. Wt. 117·7. Labelled as collected by Conolly at Kanauj, but Prinsep says he got it from Miss Watson. Figured in P.E. pl. xxiii. 31, and Records, fig. 4 of plate.

B. Two specimens.

Variety β. With pedestal under सि.

B. One specimen.

W.T. One specimen.

Mr. Rivett-Carnac, Sir A. Cunningham, and the late Sir E. C. Bayley's cabinet each possess one specimen of the type, but I have not noted to which variety these coins belong. The Freeling collection included one example, wt. 115 (J.A.S.B. vol. xxiv. p. 498). The Stacy cabinet (P.E. pl. xxiii. p. 32), and the Bush cabinet (J.A.S.B. vol. xxiv. p. 499) also possessed a specimen each.

Several examples were included in the Tânḍâ hoard, where they were associated with coins of Chandra Gupta I. and Kâcha, and Battle-axe coins of Samudra Gupta.

The meaning of the syllable *Si* on the obverse has not yet been explained. The same syllable is found on the footstool in the Lyrist type of Samudra Gupta, and on an unpublished Indo-Scythian coin belonging to Sir A. Cunningham. The word *parâkrama* on the reverse is a favourite with Samudra Gupta, and the wording of the obverse legend, as far as it has been deciphered, resembles the language used in the Allâhâbâd Pillar inscription to describe his achievements. We know from the inscriptions that he actually performed the *Aśwamedha* or horse sacrifice, as claiming the position of lord paramount of India. These facts, especially when considered in connection with the composition of the Tânḍâ hoard, establish beyond doubt that the *Aśwamedha* pieces were issued by Samudra Gupta. A coin of similar type, with the horse to the right, is assigned to Kumâra Gupta (*post*, p. 110). Samudra's *Aśwamedha* pieces agree in weight with his

SAMUDRA GUPTA—*continued.*

ordinary coinage, but were evidently struck as commemorative medals, and were probably distributed to the Brahmans, who assisted in the sacrifice. For remarks on the *Aśwamedha* and the titles of Samudra Gupta see Corpus Inscriptionum Indicarum, vol. iii. pp. 27–28.

I think that the *Aśwamedha* medals must have been struck early in his reign.

Lyrist Type.

Obv. King, wearing close cap and tight drawers, to front, with head turned to l., seated on high-backed couch, over edge of which his feet are dangling. He is playing an Indian lyre, (*vīṇâ*), which rests on his lap.

On footstool the syllable सि, *Si*, except in one coin. Marginal legend महाराजाधिराज श्री समुद्र गुप्तः, *mahârâjâdhirâja S'rî Samudra Guptaḥ*, 'the sovereign of Mahârâjâs, S'rî Samudra Gupta.'

Rev. Goddess, turned to l., seated on Indian wicker stool (*moṛhâ*), holding in r. hand fillet, and in l. cornucopiæ. Between figure and legend generally a vertical line or mace.

Legend in r. field समुद्र गुप्तः, *Samudra Guptaḥ*. Mon. sometimes wanting.

References and Remarks.—Variety a. Broad thin coins with footstool and 'Si.'

B.M. Eden. Broad thin coin, design in very low relief. Diameter ·91. No mon. Wt. 111. On obv. king's name is written समुंद्र *Sarmudra*. (Pl. I. Fig. 5.)

B.M. Prinsep. No mon. Wt. 119·5. Is probably the coin from Stacy collection figured in P.E. pl. xxiii. 26. A similar coin is figured in As. Res. xvii. pl. i. 19.

A.G. Wt. 117·4. From Oudh. Resembles B.M. coins.

A.C. 3 specimens.

Bharsar hoard, No. 2. Mon. 8*a*. Wt. 12·2. (J.A.S.B. vol. xxi. pp. 392, 396, pl. xii. 5.)

H. One specimen from Pargana Nawâbganj in Gonḍâ District, Oudh, opposite Ajodhyâ.

W.T. Vertical line or mace on rev. wanting.

SAMUDRA GUPTA—*continued.*

Variety β. Thick coins, without footstool or 'Si.'

B.M. **I.O.** Diameter ·72. Wt. 120·7. Rudely executed, and the attitude of the king differs from that shown in variety *a*. Obv. legend imperfect. Rev. legend as in *a*. Mon. 11. At present unique. (Pl. I. Fig. 6.)

These Lyrist coins, excepting the unique India Office example of variety *β*, like the Aśwamedha pieces, have the appearance of medals rather than of ordinary coins. They commemorate Samudra Gupta's musical accomplishments, which are eulogized in the Allâhâbâd Pillar inscription, and it seems probable that this very peculiar coinage was issued to commemorate some special festival. Variety *a* is finely executed in low relief, and the diameter is greater than that of any other type, except the fine and unique Retreating Lion coin of Chandra Gupta II., which also measures ·91.

The India Office specimen of variety *β* is very coarsely designed and executed, but does not look like a forgery. I cannot give any certain explanation of its peculiarities. Its general appearance is totally different from that of the variety *a* coins, and its style is rather that of the late coins of Kumâra Gupta and Skanda Gupta. Perhaps it was struck in some outlying province.

The unexplained syllable *Si* on the obverse of variety *a* obviously connects this type with the Aśwamedha medals. Very likely the Lyrist medals were struck on the same occasion as the Aśwamedha ones.

The goddess seated on the wicker stool makes her first appearance on this type.

JAVELIN TYPE.

Obv. King standing (to l. in varieties *a* and *γ*, to r. in variety *β*), dressed in tailed coat and leggings in Indo-Scythian style, with r. hand (l. hand in variety *β*) casting incense on a small fire altar, and with l. arm (r. arm in variety *β*) resting on spear or javelin. Bird standard, generally adorned with pennons, behind the arm, which does not hold the javelin.

SAMUDRA GUPTA—*continued.*

In variety *a*, स मु द्र *Samudra* under l. arm.

In variety *β* the same legend under king's r. arm, which holds the javelin.

In variety *γ*, स मु द्र | गु प्त *Samudra Gupta,* under l. arm.

Marginal legend, sometimes following margin, and sometimes parallel to javelin,[1] समर शत वितत विजयो जितरि [or रे] परदेवो जयति, *Samara śata vitata vijayo jita ri* [or *re*] *pa ra devo jayati,* 'his majesty victorious in a hundred widely extended [*or* various] battles, having conquered [his enemies] is victorious.'

Rev. Lakshmî, facing front, seated on raised throne with four lathe-turned legs, her feet resting on a footstool, r. hand holding fillet, l. arm grasping cornucopiæ. Legend near r. margin पराक्रमः, *parâkramaḥ,* 'prowess *or* might.' Mon.

The reverse is the same in all varieties.

References and Remarks.—Variety a. King to l. 'Samudra' under l. arm.

B.M. **Prinsep.** Mon. 8*a*. Wt. 117·8. (Pl. I. Fig. 7.)

B.M. **Prinsep.** Mon. 3*a*. Wt. 114. From cabinet of Col. Smith of Patna, figured in P.E. pl. xxii. 17.

B.M. **Twisden.** Mon. 20*a*. Wt. 117·4.

B.M. **Twisden.** Mon. 3*a*. Wt. 117·8.

B.M. **I.O. No. 1.** Mon. 3*a*. Wt. 114·4. In poor condition.

B.M. **I.O. No. 2.** Mon. 3*a*. Wt. 108·2. ,,

B.M. **I.O. No. 3.** Mon. 4*c*. Wt. 113·4. ,,

B.M. **I.O. No. 4.** Mon. 4*c*. Wt. 114·8. ,,

B.M. **I.O. No. 5.** Mon. 22. Wt. 118·6. ,,

B.M. **Eden.** Mon. 4*c*. Wt. 119·2. In fine condition. Legend parallel to javelin. (Pl. I. Fig. 8.)

[1] Formerly I classed as a separate variety the coins of which the legend is parallel to the javelin, but the distinction is not well marked in some of the Bodleian examples, and I have now combined in one class the coins formerly arranged as varieties 1 and 3.

SAMUDRA GUPTA—*continued.*

B. 10 specimens. Mons. *4c, 4d, 6a, 8a, 8b, 19c.*

S. 4 specimens. Mons. *3a, 4c, 19a.*

A.C. 4 specimens.

A.G. 2 specimens, both from Oudh. Mons. *8a* and *4b*. Wts. 114·5 and 116·5.

A.S.B. 2 specimens.

H. 2 specimens, from hoard found in mound on Râptî river in pargana Atraula of Goṇḍâ District, Oudh. Mr. Boys, B.C.S., has a specimen from same hoard.

Bharsar hoard. No. 4 of Samudra. Mon. *3a.* Wt. 117.

Hûglî hoard. 1 specimen.

W.T. 3 specimens.

See A.A. pl. xviii. 6, 9; As. Res. vol. xvii. pl. i. 7; P.E. pl. xxii. 16, 17, and pl. xxix. 14; J.A.S.B. vol. xxi. p. 396.

Variety β. King to r., javelin in r. hand, and name 'Samudra' under r. arm.

As. Res. xvii. plate i. 5. Mon. imperfect.

Variety γ. King to l., 'Samudra Gupta' under l. arm.

B.M. Bush. Mon. *4c.* Wt. 119·3. In fine condition. (Pl. I. Fig. 9.)

Bharsar hoard. No. 5 of Samudra. Mon. *3a.* Wt. 114. (J.A.S.B. vol. xxi. p. 396.)

A.C. One specimen.

C. Wt. 117·6 Obtained at Mathurâ.

The device of the obverse evidently connects this type with the coins of Kâcha, which appear to be contemporary, and with the Indo-Scythian coinages. The Javelin coins may have been struck at any period of Samudra Gupta's reign. They certainly constituted his principal issue. The coins of variety *a* are the commonest of all the Gupta gold coins, except the Archer type, Class II. A., of Chandra Gupta II. I have enumerated more than forty specimens, and have no doubt that many more exist. Variety *β* is known only from the coin figured in the Asiatic Researches. Variety *γ* seems to be very scarce. I have seen only three specimens, as enumerated above. The fourth was included in the Bharsar hoard, but I do not know what became of the coins from that hoard.

SAMUDRA GUPTA—*continued.*

The reading of the obverse legend was settled by Mr. Fleet. One word, which should be a substantive, has not yet been deciphered. It looks like *repara* or *ripara* on the coin figured in Pl. I. Fig. 9.

Line 17 of the Allâhâbâd Pillar inscription commemorates Samudra Gupta's conquests in similar language.[1]

The tautological form of expression is common in the legends of the Gupta coins.

The first four forms of the letter *m* given on p. 35 *ante*, all occur in the legends of coins of this type, different forms being often used on a single coin. The coins figured (Pl. I. Fig. 7–9) illustrate some of the alphabetical variations. The square form of *t*, scarcely distinguishable from *ś*, shown in Fig. 8, is noticeable, but not very uncommon.

Archer Type.

Obv. King standing to l., with l. arm resting on bow, and r. hand, either holding arrow (variety *a*), or offering incense on altar (variety *β*). Bird standard adorned with pennons behind r. arm. Under l. arm स / मु / द्र *Samudra.*

Marginal legend not fully deciphered, but it contains the words देव विजय . . . अप्रतिरथ विजित्य क्षितिमव [जित्य], *deva vijaya . . . apratiratha vijitya kshitim ava[jitya].*

Rev. Throned goddess (Lakshmî) with fillet and cornucopiæ, as in Javelin type.

Legend in variety *a* is अप्रतिरथः, *apratirathaḥ*, 'invincible in his war-chariot'; and variety *β* is पराक्रमः, *parâkramaḥ*, as in Javelin type. Mon.

References and Remarks.—Variety a. King holding arrow. Rev. legend 'apratirathaḥ.'

B.M. Eden. Mon. 4*c*. Wt. 118. Well-executed coin in fine condition. (Pl. I. Fig. 10.)

B.M. Prinsep. Mon. 21 (irregular). Wt. 117·4. Dug up

[1] Corpus Inscr. Ind. vol. iii. p. 12, note 2.

SAMUDRA GUPTA—*continued.*

at Jaunpur by Tregear, along with Archer coin, class I., of Chandra Gupta II.

B.M. **I.O.** Mon. 22 (irregular). Wt. 120. Figured in A.A. pl. xviii. 8.

B. Mon. 22*b*.

A.G. Two specimens from Oudh. Mons. indistinct. Wt. 117·1 and 119·2.

A.C. One specimen.

A.A. Pl. xviii. 7. From Swiney collection. Mon. 19*a*.

Variety β. King sacrificing at altar. Rev. legend 'parâkramaḥ.'

Bharsar hoard. No. 1 (two specimens) and No. 3 of Samudra Gupta. Wts. 110, 114, and 110.

A scarce type. I have never seen a specimen of variety β, which is known only from the three examples in the Bharsar hoard, not now forthcoming. This variety is identical with the Javelin type, except that the king holds a bow instead of a javelin. The epithet *apratiratha*, 'invincible in his war-chariot,' is applied to Samudra Gupta in the Allâhâbâd Pillar inscription. The obv. legend has not been fully made out, but is one of the usual boasts of having conquered the earth. The obv. device served as the model for all the subsequent Archer coinages, but is distinctly superior to them in execution.

Battle-axe Type.

Obv. King, wearing tailed coat, standing, leaning on battle-axe. An attendant supports a standard tipped with a crescent. In variety α and β king is to l., and attendant in l. field. In variety γ king is to r., and attendant in r. field. In varieties α and γ under king's arm स मु द्र *Samudra*. In variety β the syllable कृ, *Kṛi*, is under his arm.

Marginal legend in varieties α and γ कृतान्त परशु राजाधिराज, *Kṛitânta paraśu râjâdhirâja*, 'the sovereign armed with the axe of Kṛitânta.' In variety β it seems in part to differ.

SAMUDRA GUPTA—*continued.*

Rev. Lakshmî on throne, facing front, with feet on lotus-flower. Fillet in r. hand, cornucopiæ in l. arm. Throne sometimes indistinct. Legend कृतान्त परशु, *Kṛitânta paraśu*, 'the battle-axe of Kṛitânta.' Mon.

References and Remarks.—Variety a. King to l., 'Samudra' under arm.

B.M. Bush. Mon. 6*a*. Wt. 123·4. Throne indistinct. (Pl. I. Fig. 11.) A star and second crescent above the crescent-tipped standard.

B.M. Thomas. Throne indistinct, or wanting. Mon. 6*a*. Wt. 117.

B.M. Prinsep. A star above crescent-tipped standard. On rev. an axe-head attached to back of throne. Mon. 6*a*. Wt. 116·7. Obtained by Conolly at Kanauj. Figured in P.E. xxiii. pl. 23.

A.S.B. and **A.C.** One specimen each.

Tâṇḍâ hoard. Several specimens.

The coin figured in P.E. pl. xxix. 11 is one of two obtained by Cunningham at Benares. Prinsep had a third similar.

Variety β.—King to l. 'Kṛi' under arm.

B.M. Eden. Obv. legend on l. margin looks like जजतज, *jajataja*. On r. margin it is कृतन्त प, *Kṛitanta pa-*. No axe on rev. Mon. 3*a*. Wt. 117·7. (Pl. I. Fig. 12.)

Variety γ. King to r.; attendant in r. field.

Swiney collection. Figured in A.A. pl. xviii. 10. No rev. battle-axe. Mon. 3*a*.

A scarce type. Varieties β and γ are each known from a single specimen only. I do not know what has become of the Swiney example of the latter. This type is evidently intended to represent Samudra Gupta as an incarnation of Yama, the god of Death, under his name Kṛitânta, 'he that maketh an end.' We may conjecture that the coins were struck to commemorate some of the king's numerous conquests, which are celebrated in detail in the Allâhâbâd Pillar inscription. The crescent-tipped standard of the obv. is found on the rev. of his Tiger type.

KÂCHA (? = SAMUDRA GUPTA).

STANDARD TYPE.

Obv. King to l., standing, in dress and pose almost exactly the same as on the Javelin coins of Samudra Gupta. His l. arm rests on a standard with pennons, bearing a rayed wheel-like symbol. With his r. hand he casts incense on a small altar.

Under l. arm का : च '*Kâcha.*'

Marginal legend काचो गामवजित्य कर्मभिरुत्तमैर्जयति, *Kâcha, gâm avajitya, karmabhir uttamair jayati*, 'Kâcha, having subdued the earth, by excellent deeds is victorious.'

Rev. Goddess (Lakshmî), standing to l., clad in long robe, holding lotus-flower in r. hand, and grasping cornucopiæ in l. arm.

Legend near r. margin, सर्वराजोच्छेत्ता *sarvarâjochchhettâ*, 'exterminator of all râjâs.'

References and Remarks.

B.M. **Prinsep.** Mon. 2. Wt. 115·2. (Pl. I. Fig. 3.)

B.M. **Eden.** Two specimens. Wts. 111 and 115·6 respectively. Both have same mon. 4*a*.

The coin weighing 115·6 is figured as figure 1 of plate in Records, and may be the coin figured in A.A. pl. xviii. 4.

B. **No. 678.** Mon. 1. From Tregear collection, and figured in P.E. pl. xxix. 12.

B. **No. 679.** Mon. 2*b*.

A.C. 3 specimens.

A.S.B. 1 specimen.

W.T. 2 specimens. Wt. of one is 118.

C. Wt. 125·8.

Tâṇḍâ hoard. One or more specimens.

Bush, **Stacy**, and **Freeling** cabinets—one each. The late **Mr. Gibbs** also had one.

These coins were formerly attributed to Ghaṭotkacha, the second prince of the Gupta dynasty, and in my previous publication I followed Prinsep and Thomas in so assigning them. But Mr. Fleet has since proved that they cannot have been struck by Ghaṭotkacha, and there is no reason

KÂCHA (?=SAMUDRA GUPTA)—*continued.*

whatever for supposing that they were.[1] The attribution was suggested by the misreading of Kacha for Kâcha under the King's arm and a second mislection of the obv. marginal legend by Prinsep. The better-preserved examples show beyond all doubt that the name under the king's arm is Kâcha, with the long vowel. Even if the name could be read Kacha, which it cannot be, the syllables Kacha could not stand alone, because the name Ghaṭotkacha in the Sanskritized form, in which alone it has come down to us, is a compound of *ghaṭa* and *utkacha*, the latter word being itself a compound of *ut* and *kacha*, and used adjectivally. Moreover, Ghaṭotkacha, like his father Gupta, assumed only the subordinate title of Mahârâjâ, and it was not the practice of Mahârâjâs to coin gold money, at all events, even if they may have coined sometimes in other metals. The name Kâcha has not yet been found in any of the Gupta inscriptions, but the style and legends of the coins under discussion forbid us to doubt that they were struck by a Gupta king. The standing goddess on the reverse is unmistakeably executed in the same style of art as the similar figures on the Tiger and Aśwamedha coins of Samudra Gupta, and the king's name is inserted under his arm on the obv. in the manner usual on the Gupta coins. The king's figure and attitude are identical with those of Samudra Gupta on the Javelin type. The epithet 'exterminator of all râjâs' occurs five times in the Gupta inscriptions, in four of which it is certainly applied to Samudra Gupta, and in the fifth instance it probably refers to him.[2] The formula *gâm avajitya* recurs on the Swordsman coins of Kumâra Gupta, and several Gupta types have legends identical in meaning, though not exactly in expression. In the Tâṇḍâ hoard coins of Kâcha were

[1] Ind. Ant. vol. xiv. p. 96 (March and June, 1885); Corpus Inscr. Ind. vol. iii. p. 27, note 4.

[2] Ind. Ant. vol. xiv. p. 95. Mr. Fleet observes that the name Kâcha is of rare occurrence, but that two kings or chieftains of the name are mentioned in an inscription of the fifth or sixth century A.D. in the Ajaṇṭâ caves, published in Arch. Survey of Western India, vol. iv. p. 130. The name Kacha, with the short vowel, occurs in the Mahâbhârata. See Dowson's Classical Dictionary of Hindu Mythology, etc., *sub voce.*

KÂCHA (?=SAMUDRA GUPTA)—*continued.*

found associated with coins of the Aśwamedha and Battle-axe types of Samudra Gupta, and with the King and Queen types of his father Chandra Gupta I. The alphabet of the legends agrees with that of Samudra Gupta's coinage. The entire evidence therefore points directly to the conclusion that the Kâcha coins were struck by a member of the Gupta dynasty, and that they are contemporaneous with the coins of Samudra Gupta. The further inference that they were issued by Samudra Gupta himself is unavoidable, because there is no room for a co-ordinate independent contemporary, and Samudra's and Kâcha's coinages are found together, and were evidently current in the same region.

The rayed emblem or wheel surmounting the standard on the obv. most likely symbolizes the sun. The Gupta symbolism is all Hindu. A similar rayed symbol is found detached on the Wheel variety of the Archer coins of Chandra Gupta II.

CHANDRA GUPTA II.

Couch Type.

Obv. King wearing waistcloth, seated on couch, with r. leg tucked up, and l. foot resting on ground. His l. hand rests upon the couch, the r. hand is upraised empty.

Marginal legend देव श्री [महाराजा] धिराज श्री च[न्द्र] गुप्तः, *deva S'rî [mahârâjâ]dhirâja S'rî Cha[ndra] Guptaḥ*, 'his majesty, the fortunate (*S'rî*) sovereign of Mahârâjas, S'rî Chandra Gupta.' Also two or three obscure characters below couch.

Rev. Throned goddess (Lakshmî), holding fillet in r. hand and flower in l. hand.

Legend श्री विक्रमः, *S'rî Vikramaḥ.* Mon.

References and Remarks.

B.M. Mon. 3*a*. Wt. 114·7. Condition worn. (Pl. I. Fig. 13.)

This type is known to us from the one coin only. I am indebted to Sir A. Cunningham for the information that a rude engraving of the same coin, which then belonged to

CHANDRA GUPTA II.—*continued.*

a Dr. Frazer, was published so far back as 1797. This engraving will be found at p. 425, vol. ii. of a scarce book, a copy of which is in the library of the Royal Asiatic Society, London. The full title is "The Oriental Collections, consisting of Original Essays and Dissertations, Translations and Miscellaneous Papers; Illustrating the History and Antiquities, the Arts, Sciences, and Literature of Asia." Two volumes, quarto, N.D. Published by subscription for Cadell and Davies, Strand. The preface is dated 1797.

The king's attitude on the obv. is very nearly the same as that of Samudra Gupta in his Lyrist type, but here there is no lyre. The legends indicate that the coin must be assigned to Chandra Gupta II., and not to his grandfather. Śrî Vikrama is the title specially affected by Chandra Gupta II.[1] The obv. legend is identical with that of the Archer coins of Chandra Gupta II. The throned goddess of the rev. points to an early period of his reign. The later coins place the goddess on a lotus-flower seat.

Javelin Type.

Obv. and *rev.* As described below.

References and Remarks.

This type is known only from a unique coin, described by Dr. Hoernlé as follows:

Boys. "About two months ago I received from Mr. Henry S. Boys, B.C.S., in Lucknow, for decipherment, a gold Gupta coin, which he had obtained at Badaulí, about 25 miles from Ajudhyá. It is of a quite new type, and apparently unique. It is of somewhat coarse workmanship, though not more so than many other Gupta coins of well-known types, and is undoubtedly genuine, as it was bought of a common man at a little above its intrinsic value. Weight 112·5 grains. (See Pl. V. Fig 3.)

"*Obv.* King standing in the same posture as on Samudra Gupta's

[1] "With regard to the meaning of *Vikrama*, which is properly 'heroism,' it may be observed that it is often used in a way where 'king' or 'hero' alone can be signified by it; thus *Vikramâditya* is as often called simply *Vikrama* as not. . . The word is applied also attributively as *Dîpakarṇir iti khyâto râjâ bhûd râjya-vikramaḥ*, 'There was a king named Dîpakarṇi, the Vikrama of the realm.'"—(Wilson, Specimens of the Theatre of the Hindus, vol. i. p. 196.)

CHANDRA GUPTA II.—*continued.*

coins of the "Javelin" type (see Mr. Smith's Catalogue, J.A.S.B. vol. liii. part i. p. 172). King standing to left, dressed in be-jewelled close-fitting tail coat, trousers, and tall pointed cap, left arm resting on javelin, right hand casting incense on a small altar in left field; behind right arm the bird standard; corona round the head. Under the king's left arm, within the field, **चन्द्र** *chandra*; along the left hand margin **पर॰ म॰ भग॰** *para. ma. bhaga*; along the right hand margin **प्रवीरः गुप्त** *praviraḥ Gupta.* The obverse is imperfectly struck; it looks as if the coin slipped on the die; most of the letters appear double, slightly overlapping each other; still they are all tolerably distinct, except **गुप्त** *gupta*, the **प** *p* of which is wanting. The marginal legend consists of abbreviated words, which I take to be in full *paramabhágavatapravíraḥ Chandra Guptaḥ, i.e.* 'The most devoted worshipper of Vishṇu, the mighty Chandra Gupta.' The circle is a well-known mark of abbreviation; its being used three times would seem to indicate three abbreviated words; but the first circle may be redundant; otherwise the phrase might be *parama-mahá-* (or *mahad-*)*bhágavata.*

"*Rev.* King and queen sitting on a couch, facing each other. The king sits on the right side, right leg drawn up on the couch, and his right hand holding up and apparently showing to the queen a cup, shaped somewhat like a modern champagne glass. The queen sits on the left-side margin of the couch, with both legs down, supporting herself with the right arm on the corner of the couch, and her left arm a-kimbo. Both figures are dressed in lower garments (*dhotis*), the king in short ones reaching to above the knees, the queen in long ones coming down to below the knees. Both wear jewels in their hair and ears, also bracelets, the king also a necklace, and the queen anklets. There is a sort of corona round the king's head. The scene seems to represent a drinking bout, similar to what may be seen on old Buddhist sculptures. On the margin, behind the queen, **श्री वि** *śri vi*, similarly behind the king, **क्रमः** *kramaḥ*; that is **श्री विक्रमः** *S'ri Vikramaḥ.*

"It is doubtful whether this coin should be attributed to Chandra Gupta I. or Chandra Gupta II. The only point, however, which really seems to favour the attribution to the latter king, is the reverse legend *S'rí Vikramaḥ*, which has hitherto been only found on coins of that king. The words *paramabhágavata* (if correct) have also been met with on coins of the same king (see J.A.S.B.,

CHANDRA GUPTA II.—*continued.*

vol. liii. pp. 180, 182). But another, and more striking peculiarity points rather to an older date for the coin, and to Chandra I. as its issuer. The king's figure on the obverse has a decidedly antique look. It closely resembles that on the early coins of the so-called Ghaṭot-kacha, and of Chandra Gupta I. (*ibid.* plate ii. figs 1–4). The reverse device of 'King and Queen,' too, has hitherto been only observed on coins of Chandra Gupta I. and of Skanda Gupta (see *ibid.* pp. 129, 171). If the coin should be attributed to Chandra Gupta II., we must assume that, on some of his coins, he reverted to the more antique obverse device of his early predecessors. On the other hand, as hitherto only one type (King and Queen) of coin of Chandra Gupta I. has been discovered, it is impossible to assert, that he might not have used the legend *S'rî Vikramaḥ* on other coins. On the whole, the ascription to Chandra Gupta I. appears to me the more probable one."—Proc.A.S.B. for 1888, pl. v. 3.

This type is the most curious addition made for a long time past to the varied series of Gupta coin types. The collotype accompanying Dr. Hoernlé's paper is unfortunately too indistinct to reproduce. I cannot accept his theory that the so-called circles in the obverse legend indicate abbreviations. Such abbreviations are unknown on the Gupta coins, and the 'circles' are evidently letters. The syllable *ma* on the l. obv. margin seems to me to be followed by the word '*Chandra*,' the second 'circle' being the character च *Cha*. On the r. margin the word either प्रवीरः or प्रवरः, *pravîraḥ* or *pravaraḥ*, appears distinct. The name Chandra under the king's arm on obv. is certain, and I think the word '*Gupta*' is arranged vertically outside the javelin.

The rev. legend is as read by Dr. Hoernlé. The object, which he interprets as the bowl of the 'champagne-glass,' looks to me like part of the wheel symbol.

The reverse device is most peculiar, and according to the analogy of the other types, ought to be the obverse.

The king's figure recalls the Couch type.

I think it more probable that the coin belongs to the reign of Chandra Gupta II. than to that of his grandfather.

CHANDRA GUPTA II.—*continued.*

Archer Type.

Obv. King wearing tailed coat, standing, grasping a bow in one hand, and holding an arrow in the other. The name चन्द्र, *Chandra*, under the bow arm, and the bird standard behind the other arm. Sometimes a wheel or crescent above king's shoulder.

Marginal legend of Class I. and Class II. A. देव श्री महाराजाधिराज श्री चन्द्र गुप्तः, *deva S'rî mahârâjâdhirâja S'rî Chandra Guptaḥ*, 'his majesty, the fortunate (*S'rî*) sovereign of mahârâjâs, S'rî Chandra Gupta.'

Marginal legend of Class II. B. not read.

Rev. *Class I.* Goddess (Lakshmî) seated on throne, holding in r. hand fillet, and in l. cornucopiæ, or flower.

Class II. Goddess (Lakshmî) seated cross-legged on lotus-flower, holding in r. hand fillet, and in l. hand lotus-flower.

Legend of Class I. and Class II. A. श्री विक्रमः, *S'rî Vikramaḥ.* The क *k* is often doubled.

In Class II. B. legend seems to include the title Vikramâditya. Mon.

References and Remarks.

Class I. Throne Reverse. Wt. normal.

Variety a. Bow-string inwards.

A.G. Mon. 16. Wt. 113·2. From Oudh.

C. Wt. 118·9.

Tregear. Mon. 21. Dug up at Jaichandra's Mahal, Jaunpur, along with an Archer coin of Samudra Gupta, and figured in P.E. pl. xxiii. 18. P.E. pl. xxix. 13 figures "a very perfect example from Cunningham's cabinet, procured at Mirzâpur." Mon. 3*a*. The goddess on this coin is shown as holding a flower, not a cornucopiæ. This may be the coin now in possession of A. C.

B. Mon. 19*d*.

Variety β. Bow-string outwards.

B.M. I.O. No. 8. Mon. 4*c*. Wt. 120·9. (Pl. I. Fig. 14.) Seems to be the coin from Barhal in Gorakhpur (J.A.S.B. vol. xxiv. p. 499).

CHANDRA GUPTA II.—*continued.*

M., mlvii. Mon. 4*c*. Wt. 118·5.

B. Mon. 4*c*.

Class II. Lotus-flower seat Reverse.

A. Coins of normal weight, averaging about 123 grains.

Variety a. King to l. Bow in l. hand. No wheel or crescent over shoulder.

B.M. Eden. Two *k*s in rev. legend. Mon. 7*a*. Wt. 124·3. In fine condition. (Pl. I. Fig. 15.)

B.M. Swiney. Mon. 10*b*. Wt. 124·6. In fine condition.

B.M. Marsden, ml. Mon. 20*a*. Wt. 124·5.

B.M. Brind. Mon. 10*a*. Wt. 117·8.

B.M. Prinsep. Mon. 3*b*. Wt. 121·7.

B.M. T. Mon. 8*b*. Wt. 126·3.

B.M. Yeames No. 4. Mon. 8*b*. Wt. 124·7.

B.M. Yeames No. 5. Mon. 1. Wt. 119·2.

B.M. Yeames No. 6. Mon. 10*a*. Wt. 121·8.

B.M. I.O. No. 3. Mon. 24. Wt. 125·5.

B.M. I.O. No. 4. Mon. 3*b*. Wt. 123.

B.M. I.O. No. 5. Mon. 24. Wt. 127·6.

B.M. I.O. No. 6. Mon. 8*a*. Wt. 119·7.

B.M. I.O. No. 7. Mon. 17*a*. Wt. 126·5.

B. Ten specimens, Nos. 697–706. No. 706 has the rare mon. 17*c*.

A.S.B. Eight specimens, besides one of base metal, which probably belongs to the heavy class, B.

Bastî hoard. Nine specimens. Mons. 8*a*, 8*b*, 10*b*, and 19*b*.

A.C. Five specimens.

It would be superfluous to attempt to enumerate all the specimens of this variety.

Variety β. As variety a, with a wheel over king's r. shoulder.

B.M. I.O. No. 9. Mon. 18. Wt. 132·5. (Pl. I. Fig. 16.)

B.M. I.O. No. 10. Mon. 17*b*. Wt. 130·5.

B.M. I.O. No. 13. Mon. 8*a*. Wt. 129·5.

A.G. Mon. lost. Wt. 130·4. Rude coin, from Oudh. An indistinct object seems to take the place of the wheel.

Bharsar hoard. No. 2 of Chandra Gupta (two specimens). Mon. 15. Wt. 130 (J.A.S.B. vol. xxi. p. 394, pl. xii. 1).

C. Wt. 125·75.

6

CHANDRA GUPTA II.—*continued.*

Variety γ. As variety β, but a crescent in place of wheel.

B.M. I.O. No. 11. Mon. 8*a*. Wt. 126·6. Worn.

B.M. I.O. No. 12. Mon. 8*b*. Wt. 126·7. Worn.

Bharsar hoard. No. 3 of Chandra Gupta (two specimens). Mon. 8*a*. Wt. 126. (J.A.S.B. xxi. pl. xii. 2.)

Variety δ. King to r. Bow in r. hand, and name under r. arm.

B.M. I.O. No. 1. Mon. 8*a*. Wt. 118·4. Worn. (Pl. II. Fig. 1.)

Bharsar hoard. No. 4 of Chandra Gupta. Mon. 8*a*. Wt. 112. (J.A.S.B. xxi. pl. xii. 3.)

Variety ε. King to r. Bow in l. hand, and name under l. arm.

B.M. I.O. No. 2. Mon. 4*c*. Wt. 122·3.

A.S.B. Seemingly the coin from Bulandshahr, mentioned in Proc. A.S.B. April, 1879.

B. Coins of *suvarṇa* standard, with average weight of about 146 grains, king to l.

B.M. Marsden, mlvi. *Chandra* under king's l. arm, with a crescent above the name. भा *bhá* between king's legs. Rev. legend, श्री देव, . . . *S'rí Deva* . . . (Pl. II. Fig. 2.) Mon. indistinct. Wt. 144·5.

B.M. Marsden, mli. Resembles last. Rev. legend [विक्रमा]दित्य, [*Vikramá*]*ditya*. Mon. 19*a*. Wt. 148.

B.M. T. Wt. 144·7.

A.G. Rev. legend श्री विक्रम, *S'rí Vikrama*. Mon. imperfect. Wt. 144·5. Metal impure, from Oudh.

C. Wt. 146·25.

The Archer type of Chandra Gupta is the form in which the most extensive issues of the Gupta gold coinage took place. Specimens of Class II. A. *a*, are met with in such numbers that they may be said to be common, an epithet which cannot well be applied to any other set of Gupta coins, except perhaps to the Javelin coins of Samudra Gupta.

Class I., with the throned goddess on the reverse, is imitated from the Archer type of Samudra Gupta, but with marked deterioration in artistic execution. The coins of both varieties of this class are rare, and evidently belong to an

CHANDRA GUPTA II.—*continued.*

early period of the reign of Chandra Gupta II. The throned goddess does not again appear on the Gupta coinage.

The figure of the goddess Lakshmî, seated cross-legged on an open lotus-flower, which is the reverse device employed in Class II., had already made its appearance on some specimens of the Battle-axe coins of Samudra Gupta, which may be regarded as his latest issue. From the time that it was adopted by Chandra Gupta II., it became and long remained the favourite device in Northern India, suffering great degradation in course of time. Even in the case of coins which seem to have been struck in the reign of Chandra Gupta II., the execution of the device varies much, and is sometimes very barbarous.

The heavy coins (Class II. B.), which seem to have been struck to the *suvarṇa* standard of 146 grains, agree generally in device with the common Class II. A. *a*, but seem to differ in reverse legend. The name under the king's arm has a crescent above it, as in the other heavy types. The execution of these heavy coins of Chandra is decidedly barbarous, but so is that of many specimens of his coinage of normal weight. The latter are, also, frequently composed of very impure metal. Neither in style nor fabric is there much to choose between the better heavy and the worse light coins, and I am now inclined to assign the heavy coins, or most of them, which bear the name of Chandra, to the reign of Chandra Gupta II. They sometimes occur in base metal, and these specimens may be posthumous imitations. The better specimens may represent a provincial coinage. In my former publication I placed all these heavy coins in a supplement, but they are plainly Gupta coins, and I know of no later prince to whom they can be attributed. The genealogy of the local Gupta dynasty of Magadha does not include a Chandra. The title Vikramâditya, which Chandra Gupta II. certainly used on his Umbrella gold pieces, and his silver and copper coins, is also used on these heavy gold coins. No single specimen shows the complete word, but comparison of

CHANDRA GUPTA II.—*continued.*

Marsden's mli. with Mr. Grant's coin establishes the reading.

The scarce varieties δ and ε differ from the normal type in the circumstance that the king is turned to the r., instead of the l. The Gupta coinage shows by many examples that figures were depicted indifferently turned to the r. or l.

The rayed symbol, which I call a wheel, found on variety β, is probably intended for the sun, and may be compared with the similar symbol on the coins of Kâcha. The weight of these Wheel coins is generally higher than that of the other varieties, but the difference is not sufficient to warrant the inference that a different standard of weight was adopted. In variety γ a crescent takes the place of the wheel, and presumably is intended to symbolize the moon. The crescent often occurs on Gupta coins.

Horseman to Right Type.

Obv. King, proceeding to r., on prancing horse, with bow slung behind him, and, sometimes, wearing a sword. A crescent behind his head.

Marginal legend परम भागवत महाराजाधिराज श्री चन्द्र गुप्तः, *parama bhâgavata mahârâjâdhirâja S'rî Chandra Guptaḥ*; 'the most devout worshipper of the holy one, the sovereign of Mahârâjâs, S'rî Chandra Gupta.'

Rev. Goddess, to l., seated upright on wicker stool (*moṛhâ*), holding fillet in r., and lotus-flower in l. hand

Legend अजित विक्रमः, *ajita vikramaḥ*, 'of unconquered power.'

Mon. sometimes wanting.

References and Remarks.

B.M. **Prinsep, No. 1.** The *j* of the rev. legend is turned on its side. No mon. Wt. 119·7. Obtained by Bacon at Kanauj. (Pl. II. Fig. 3.)

B.M. **Prinsep, No. 2.** Wt. 118·6.

B. Mon. 19*e*.

A.S.B. Purchased (Proc. for 1884, p. 127). Wt. 130·92.

CHANDRA GUPTA II.—*continued.*

Legend nearly complete. Col. Malcolm Clerk had a similar coin, which plainly showed the king's sword.

A.C. One specimen.

W.T. One specimen. Mon. 4*e*, nearly. Wt. 120·5.

Tregear Collection. P.E. xxx. 6. Possibly the same as B.M. Prinsep, No. 2.

A.A. pl. xviii. 17. This engraving appears to be incorrect, and its peculiarities, as noted in my former catalogue, appear to be due to the engraver.

This scarce type was formerly named Lancer by me, because I was misled by Wilson's inaccurate engraving. None of the coins which I have examined has any lance. The object sticking out behind the king's back seems to be the end of a bow, as it certainly is in the Horseman to Left type.

The legends are the same as in variety *a* of the latter type.

The high weight of the A.S.B. coin is noticeable.

HORSEMAN TO LEFT TYPE.

Obv. King, proceeding to l., on prancing horse, carrying bow, half of which is visible behind him. Marginal legend of variety *a*, **परमभागवत महाराजाधिराज श्री चन्द्र गुप्तः**, *parama bhâgavata mahârâjâdhirâja S'rî Chandra Guptaḥ*, 'the devout worshipper of the holy one, the sovereign of Mahârâjas, S'rî Chandra Gupta.' The legend of variety *β* appears to be different, and consists of about twenty characters arranged all round the coin, of which I could read only **वजत**, *vajata* or *vijita*.

Rev. Goddess, seated to l. on Indian wicker stool (*moṛhâ*), holding fillet in r., and lotus-flower in l. hand.

Mon. sometimes wanting.

Legend of variety *a*, **अजित विक्रमः**, *ajita vikramaḥ*, 'of unconquered power.'

Legend of variety *β*, **क्रमाजित**, *kramâjita*, with the same meaning.

CHANDRA GUPTA II.—*continued.*

References and Remarks.—*Variety a.* *Rev. legend 'ajita vikramaḥ.'*

B. No. 710. Obv. legend clear and complete. Mon. 8*b*. In fine condition.

B. No. 711. Similar, but in inferior condition. Same mon.

S. Mon. 3*d*. Wt. 118·25. Obtained at Lucknow or Fyzabad. (Proc. A.S.B. for 1888, pl. v. 5.)

W.T. Wt. 122.

Bharsar hoard. No. 6 of Chandra Gupta. "A very perfect specimen." Wt. 122. (J.A.S.B. vol. xxi. p. 395, pl. xii. 4.)

Bharsar hoard. Described wrongly as No. 3 of Mahendra. Wt. 124. (J.A.S.B. vol. xxi. p. 399.)

Variety β. Reverse legend 'kramâjita.'

B. No. 713. Obv. legend of over 20 characters all round margin, of which only वजत legible. Rev. legend clear, क्रमाजित. No mon., but in its place seven dots and a crescent.

This type is very rare, and variety *β* is known only from the single example in the Bodleian Library. Kittoe read the epithet on the better-preserved Bharsar specimen as *parama bhaṭṭâraka*, and I formerly accepted that reading. But Mr. Sykes' coin and the two examples of variety *a* in the Bodleian Library read beyond all doubt *parama bhâgavata*. I am, therefore, of opinion that Kittoe was mistaken in his reading. Chandra Gupta II. uses the title *parama bhâgavata* on his Vikramâditya silver coins. It is also employed on the Winged Peacock silver coins of Kumâra Gupta, and both on the Winged Peacock and Bull silver coins of Skanda Gupta. The title *parama bhaṭṭâraka* has not yet been met with on any other Gupta coin, and it is unlikely, though still possible, that it was correctly read on the Bharsar coin. It was much affected by the kings of Valabhi, the successors of the Guptas in Kâthiâwâṛ, and by some members of the later Gupta dynasty of Magadha.[1]

The letters '*vajata*' or '*vijita*' on the obverse of variety *β* suggest the legend '*vijitâvanir avanipati*' etc. of the Fantail Peacock silver coins of Kumâra Gupta and his successors.

[1] Corpus Inscr. Ind. vol. iii. p. 217, etc.

CHANDRA GUPTA II.—*continued.*

The title '*kramâjita*' on the reverse of variety β has not been met with elsewhere, but is synonymous with the common epithet '*ajita vikrama.*'

Lion-Trampler Type.

Obv. King, wearing waistcloth, standing in energetic attitude, and shooting in mouth a lion, which, in varieties α, β, δ, is falling backwards with the king's foot on its belly. In variety γ the lion is standing with the king's l. foot on its back.

In varieties α, β, γ, king is turned to r., with bow in l. hand, but, in variety δ, he faces l., with bow in r. hand.

Legend not fully deciphered, but in variety δ it includes the words जयति. . . सिङ्ह विक्रम नराात [? = नरोत्तम] *jayati. . . sinha vikrama narâta* [? *narottama*], 'is victorious . . . with the power of a lion [? the best of men],' and seems to conclude with the word गुप्तः, *Guptaḥ.*

Rev. Goddess, facing front, seated on couchant lion, which faces l.

In varieties α, γ, δ, she sits cross-legged, and holds fillet in r. hand, and lotus-flower in l. hand. In variety β she sits astride, holding lotus-flower in r. hand, while the l. hand is empty.

Legend in all varieties सङ्ह विक्रमः, *sinha vikramaḥ,* 'with the power of a lion.'

Mon. generally inserted, but sometimes wanting.

References and Remarks.—Variety α. King to r. with bow in l. hand, trampling on lion's belly. Reverse goddess cross-legged, facing front.

B.M. Swiney, No. 5. Mon. 10*c*. Wt. 115·4. (Pl. II. Fig. 4.) Figured in A.A. pl. xviii. 5, but erroneously described.

B. Mon. 8*a*. From Tregear collection. Figured in P.E. pl. xxx. 1. This may be the coin with same mon. figured in Trans. R.A.S. vol. i. pl. xii. 4th series, No. 3.

W.T. Mon. 7*b*. Wt. 122.

Variety β. Obv. as in α. Rev. goddess astride on lion, with lotus-flower in r. hand, and l. hand empty.

E.C.B. No mon. Wt. 118·2. Worn.

CHANDRA GUPTA II.—*continued.*

Variety γ. King to r., with foot on back of lion, which stands with head turned round. Rev. as a.

B. Mon. 10*b*. From Tregear collection. Figured in P.E. pl. xxx. 2.

Variety δ. King to l. with bow in r. hand, trampling with r. foot on lion's belly. Rev. as a.

B. No. 726. Obv. legend जयति जय [भु] वि सिंह विक्रम नरत, *jayati jaya* [*bhu*] *vi siṅha vikrama narata*. Mon. damaged. A similar coin, from the Stacey collection, is figured in P.E. pl. xxiii. 27, on which Prinsep read the legend as विक्रम नरान म गुप्त:. Mon. 4*c*.

C. In obv. legend नरा, *narâ*, legible. No mon. Wt. 122. Obtained at Benares.

Koṭwâ hoard. 1 specimen. In obv. legend only क *k* legible. Mon. 19*b*. Rev. legend disappeared.

No. 4 of Tod's 4th Series. Mon. 20*a*. विक्रम, *Vikrama*, legible in obv. legend. (Trans. R.A.S. vol. i. pl. xii.)

A.C. has two coins of Chandra Gupta "killing lion."

All the varieties of this type are very rare. Varieties *β* and *γ* are each known from a single specimen only, and *a* is the only variety represented in the B.M.

The obv. device is an adaptation of that of the Tiger type of Samudra Gupta, and the rev. device is borrowed from the coinage of Chandra Gupta I.

The use of titles compounded with 'Vikrama' in both the obverse and reverse legends indicates that these coins, as well as the next two succeeding types, must be assigned to Chandra Gupta II. Kumâra Gupta issued closely similar coins, but they are distinguished readily by their use of the title 'Mahendra' and of the Peacock device. I do not think that anybody now disputes that the Siṅha Vikrama coins must be assigned to the reign of Chandra Gupta II.

I cannot accept as genuine the cast in the Stacy collection, which Mr. Thomas (J.A.S.B. vol. xxiv. p. 501) described as "a cast from a genuine original. *Obv.* King to r. armed with a bow, shooting a lion; legend संह विक्रम कुमार [गुप्तपरिधि] संह महेन्द्र, 'Kumâra Gupta, of might like a lion's, most

CHANDRA GUPTA II.—*continued.*

prosperous.' *Rev.* Pârvatî seated on a lion, her r. hand extends the fillet, the l., which rests upon her knee, holds a flower; Legend **सिंह महेन्द्र**, *Sinha Mahendra*; wt. 126; type P.E. pl. xxx. 1."

The legends on the cast are quite different from those on the genuine coins of Kumâra's Lion types, and the combination of titles on the cast has no parallel in any authentic coin.

Combatant Lion Type.

Obv. King, wearing waistcloth, standing, with bow in l. hand, shooting lion in mouth, but not trampling on its body. His attitude is less energetic than in the Lion-Trampler type.

Long marginal legend, almost wholly illegible.

Rev. Goddess, holding fillet in r., and lotus-flower in l. hand, seated, facing front, cross-legged on back of lion couchant to l.

Legend **सिंह विक्रमः**, *Sinha vikramaḥ*, 'with the power of a lion.' The **क** is sometimes doubled. Mon.

References and Remarks.

B.M. **Swiney, No. 4.** Mon. 10*c*. Wt. 111·4. (Pl. II. Fig. 5.)

E.C.B. Six or seven illegible characters on l. obv. margin. **-रत चन्द्र**, *-rata Chandra*, read doubtfully on r. margin. Mon. 8*b*. Wt. 120·9.

A.G. Long obv. legend of about 20 characters. Mon. 10*c*. Wt. 117·4. From Oudh.

This type is only a slight modification of the Lion-Trampler type, and, like it, is very rare. I formerly by mistake gave the reverse legend as *S'rî Vikrama*. The E.C.B. specimen has a character before the king's face, but it is probably part of the marginal legend.

The reverse is very poorly designed and executed.

Retreating Lion Type.

Obv. King standing to front, with head turned to l., wearing tight waistcloth, armlets, large earrings, and necklace. He holds in r. hand bow, and in l. an arrow pointed downwards,

CHANDRA GUPTA II.—*continued.*

having just discharged an arrow at retreating lion, which occupies l. margin, and in whose snout an arrow-head is sticking.

Legend on r. margin माहाराजाधिराजश्री, *Mahârâjâdhirâja S'rî.*

Rev. Goddess, facing front, seated on couchant lion, which faces l.; in her r. hand fillet, and in l., which rests on her hip, an expanded lotus-flower. Her r. leg is tucked up under her, the l. hangs down behind the lion's rump.

Legend श्री सिंह विक्रमः, *S'rî Sinha Vikramaḥ.* Vertical line between device and legend. Mon.

References and Remarks.

B.M. Mon. 4*c*. Wt. 123. Diameter ·92.

A fine medal-like piece of artistic design, and spirited execution (Pl. II. Fig. 6). Obtained at Kanauj by Lieutenant Conolly. Published in P.E. vol. i. pp. 27, 280, pl. xxii. 25, and in Records, p. 22, fig. 8 of plate.

This type is known only from the unique specimen in the British Museum, which happened to be the first gold Gupta coin of which Prinsep deciphered the legends. The accident that it was found at Kanauj seems to have led Prinsep to use the erroneous phrase 'the Kanauj series' for the Gupta gold coins.

In artistic merit the coin is much superior to the bulk of the Gupta coinage, and is at least equal to the best issues of Samudra Gupta. The reverse device recalls that of the King and Queen type of Chandra Gupta I. These circumstances suggest the assignment of the coin in question to that prince, but the legends show that it belongs to the reign of his grandson. There is no reason to suppose that the elder Chandra Gupta assumed the title of Sinha Vikrama. The reverse legend differs from that of the other Sinha Vikrama coins by having Śrî prefixed. The king's name is unfortunately missing, but so much of the obverse legend as was impressed on this piece is identical in form with the corresponding part of the legends of the Lyrist type of

CHANDRA GUPTA II.—*continued.*

Samudra Gupta, and the Couch and Archer types of his son, Chandra Gupta II. The obverse design is a variation of the Tiger type of Samudra Gupta, but the legend Siṅha Vikrama forbids the assignment of this coin to that king.

UMBRELLA TYPE.

Obv. King, standing, facing l., apparently bareheaded, with l. hand resting on short sword, and with r. hand casting incense on small altar.

In r. field a miniature (male or female) figure, standing on l. foot, with r. foot raised, or with l. knee bent, holds a state umbrella over the king.

Marginal legend, विक्रमादित्य क्षितिमवजित्य सुचरति, *Vikramâditya kshitim avajitya sucharati,* 'Vikramâditya, having conquered the earth, prospers.'

Rev. Standing goddess, occupying field, holding fillet in r., and lotus-flower in l. hand.

In variety *a*, she stands on a stool or pedestal, and is turned to l.

In variety *β*, she faces front, and there is no pedestal. She seems to stand on a monster.

Legend, in both varieties, विक्रमादित्यः, *Vikramâdityaḥ,* 'the sun of power.' The क्र is sometimes doubled. Mon. sometimes wanting.

References and Remarks.—Variety a. Reverse goddess to l. on pedestal.

B.M. Eden, No. 1. Mon. 8*b*. Wt. 119·3. (Pl. II. Fig. 7.)

B. Nos. 680, 682. Mon. 8*b*. क्र doubled.

B. No. 681. No mon. क्र not doubled (probably=P.E. pl. xxx. 7, from Tregear Collection).

Freeling Collection, No. 1. Wt. 121. Mon. 3*a*. (J.A.S.B. vol. xxiv. p. 492.)

Variety β. Goddess to front, standing on monster (?). *No pedestal.*

B.M. Eden, No. 2. Mon. damaged. Wt. 117·5. (Pl. II. Fig. 8.)

Bastî hoard. 1 specimen. Mon. 7*a*.

Freeling Collection, No. 2. Wt. 121. (J.A.S.B. vol. xxiv. p. 492.)

CHANDRA GUPTA II.—*continued.*

Mr. Thomas assigned this curious and rare type to the reign of the elder Chandra Gupta, and this decision can be supported by a comparison of the reverse device with the similar figures on the Tiger and Aśwamedha types of Samudra Gupta. But other considerations prove conclusively that the coins in question must be assigned, as they were by Sir E. C. Bayley, Sir A. Cunningham, and myself, to Chandra Gupta II. They bear on both sides the title Vikramâditya, which was employed by Chandra Gupta II. both on his copper and silver coins, as well as on his heavy gold Archer pieces. No one would suggest that these copper and silver pieces were struck by Chandra Gupta I. The title Vikramâditya was used by Skanda Gupta on one variety of his silver coinage, but there is no indication of its use by Chandra Gupta I. The reverse device is the only reason that can be given for assigning the coins in question to an early date, and it would indicate their ascription rather to Samudra Gupta than to his father. But there is no authority for the use of the title of Vikramâditya in connection with Samudra Gupta, whereas, although it was adopted by Skanda Gupta, it and Vikramâṅka, and other combinations of the word *vikrama,* were the favourite appellations of Chandra Gupta II. The obverse device affords a still stronger argument for the attribution of these coins to the later Chandra Gupta, inasmuch as it is substantially identical with that of the Umbrella type copper coins (Pl. IV. Figs. 8, 9), which have always been supposed to belong to the reign of Chandra Gupta II. The form of the obverse legend, *kshitim avajitya sucharati,* supports the same conclusion, because it is almost identical with the legend *gâm avajitya sucharati* of the Swordsman type of Kumâra Gupta II., son and successor of Chandra Gupta II. The obverse fire-altar occurs on the Swordsman coins of Kumâra Gupta as well as on the coins of Kâcha and Samudra Gupta, and its occurrence on these Umbrella coins consequently does not prove an early date. The Bastî hoard contained one gold Umbrella coin, associated

CHANDRA GUPTA II.—*continued.*

with nine Archer coins of Chandra Gupta II. These considerations leave no doubt on my mind that the Umbrella gold coins were struck in his reign, and not in that of his grandfather.

I formerly gave the name Swordsman and Umbrella to this type to emphasize the connection between it and the Swordsman type of Kumâra Gupta, but now use a simpler designation. The close connection between the legends of these two types has induced me to place the Umbrella coins at the end of the series of the issues of Chandra Gupta II., but this reason is not decisive, and the style of the coins perhaps indicates an earlier date. It is noticeable that the copper Umbrella coins simply describe the king as Mahârâja Śrî Chandra Gupta.

The attendant holding the umbrella on the gold coins is certainly a male, as depicted on the B.M. coins, for he is shown there as wearing top-boots. But the attendant, as shown on the Bastî coin, seems to be a female, and her attitude differs slightly from that of the figure on the B.M. coins. The sculptures at Amarâvatî would lead us to expect umbrella-holders to be females.

The No. 2 Eden coin in the B.M. (variety β) is not in sufficiently good preservation to permit of certainty as to the object on which the reverse goddess stands, but it seemed to me to be a monster, something like that on which the goddess of Samudra Gupta's Tiger type is standing.

KUMÂRA GUPTA.

Swordsman Type.

Obv. King standing, facing front, with long curly hair. He wears a close cap or turban, the usual ornaments of necklace and armlets, and apparently short drawers and top-boots. With r. hand he casts incense on altar; his l. hand rests on hilt of straight sword, which hangs from his waist. Behind r. arm, bird-standard, with pennons. Under l. elbow the syllable कु, *Ku*, with a crescent above it.

KUMÂRA GUPTA—*continued.*

Legend on l. margin lost, only *j*, and perhaps *bh*, being legible. Legend on r. margin गामवजित्य सुचरति कमार, *gâm avâjitya sucharati Kumâra*, 'having subdued the earth, Kumâra prospers.'

Rev. Goddess (Lakshmî), seated cross-legged on lotus-flower seat, holding fillet in r., and open lotus flower in l. hand.

Legend near r. margin श्री कुमार गुप्त, *S'rî Kumâra Gupta*. Mon.

References and Remarks.

B.M. Prinsep. Mon. 8*b*. Wt. 124·2. (Pl. II. Fig. 9.) Published in Records, p. 23, fig. 5 of plate.

B. Mon. 8*b*.

This remarkable type is known only from the two examples above mentioned, both of which, Sir A. Cunningham tells me, were found together in the bed of the Ganges near Patna, on the site of Pâṭaliputra, which has been mostly cut away by the river.[1] When I published my catalogue of gold coins, I was not aware of the existence of the Bodleian specimen. Both coins have the same mon. and were probably struck from a single die. Both are in good preservation. The Bodleian specimen shows that the true reading on the obv. is *gâm*, not *kshitim*. The form of obv. legend resembles that of the Umbrella coins of Chandra Gupta II., with which these Swordsman coins are also connected by the resumption of the fire-altar device, which had been previously used by Kâcha and Samudra Gupta. For these reasons I consider the Swordsman type to be the earliest issue of Kumâra Gupta. Unfortunately the title on the l. obv. margin, which corresponded to the Vikramâditya of the Umbrella coins, has been lost. The crescent over the कु, *Ku*, on the obv. is noticeable, because these Swordsman coins are of normal weight, while the crescent over the initial of the king's name is generally found on the heavy coins of *suvarṇa* standard, and not on the normal pieces. It is, however, found on some of the normal Archer coins of Kumâra Gupta. Its use

[1] Arch. Rep. vol. viii. p. 24.

KUMÂRA GUPTA—*continued.*

on coins which undoubtedly belong to Kumâra Gupta of the Early or Imperial dynasty is an indication that I am correct in the opinion which I now hold that at any rate the better executed heavy gold coins belong to the princes of the Imperial dynasty.

The figure of the king in the type under discussion is of the short stumpy form, with a peculiar bend, which is specially characteristic of the coinage of Kumâra Gupta. The artistic merit of these coins is small, but they are not inferior to some of the Archer coins of Chandra Gupta, though decidedly inferior to the Sinha Vikrama pieces.

Archer Type.

Obv. King standing to l., head bare, hair curly, r. hand extended across bird-standard, holding arrow; l. hand either resting on tip of bow, with string turned inwards (A. Class I. and B.), or grasping middle of bow, with string turned outwards (A. Class II.).

In A. Class I. under l. arm, either the syllable कु, *Ku,* with crescent above, or कुमार, *Kumâra,* arranged vertically. In B. कु, *Ku,* with crescent.

In A. Class II. कुमार, *Kumâra,* vertically, outside bow-string.

Marginal legend seems to vary widely, but the specimens are not sufficiently perfect to admit of exhaustive classification on this ground. Some have no legend at all. A considerable number read जयति महेन्द्र, *jayati Mahendra,* 'Mahendra is victorious,' but these words are part of a longer inscription.

For other legends see below.

Rev. In all varieties—goddess (Lakshmî) seated cross-legged on lotus-flower seat, holding fillet in r. hand and lotus-flower in l. But in one coin r. hand is empty, and in another instance both hands seem empty.

(A.) legend, श्री महेन्द्र:, *S'rî Mahendraḥ.*

(B.) legend, श्री कुमार गुप्त, *S'rî Kumâra Gupta.*

Mon. The mon. is omitted in one or two instances, probably by accident.

KUMÂRA GUPTA—*continued.*

References and Remarks.—A. Coins of normal weight, averaging about 125 *grains.*

Class I. Bow-string inwards; *Ku* with crescent under king's l. arm.

Variety a. Obv. legend 'jayati Mahendra,' or not read.

B.M. Eden. Mon. 8*b*. Wt. 124·7. (Pl. II. Fig. 10.)

B.M. Prinsep. Mon. illegible. Wt. 106·7. Worn.

B.M. I.O. Wt. 125·8. Rev. goddess has r. hand empty and open, with three dots below. Five dots in place of mon.

B. No. 714. Obv. legend *jayati Mah-*.

B. No. 715. Obv. legend illegible.

B. No. 716. Obv. legend illegible. Mon. 3*b*.

Bharsar hoard. Two specimens. Mon. of both 25. Wts. 123 and 124·5. (J.A.S.B. vol. xxi. p. 397.)

Jhûsî hoard. Two specimens, communicated by E.C.B.

C. One specimen, probably from same hoard.

Koṭwâ hoard. One specimen. Obv. legend includes *jayati Mahendra, Ku-*, and *râ-*.

A.S.B. Two or three specimens.

A.C. Figured in P.E. pl. xxix. 20. Mon. a form of 25. Obtained at Gayâ. A C. has a specimen now, but I do not know that it is the same. A similar coin figured in A.A. pl. xviii. 12; and another with mon. 20*a* in Trans. R.A.S. Vol. I. pl. xii. No. 1 of 4th series.

Hûglî hoard. Three specimens seem to belong to this variety.

Variety β. Obv. legend as stated below.

A.S.B. Obv. legend, as read by Dr. Hoernlé, *parama râjâdhirâja S'rî* [*Kumâra Gupta Mahen*]*dra*, the words in brackets being conjectural. A character between king's feet and '*h*' before his face. Figured in P.E. pl. xxxix. 19, and As. Res. vol. xvii. pl. i. 14.

Variety γ. Obv. legend as stated below.

A.G. Mon. 8*b*. Wt. 125. Obv. legend includes जतर, *jatara*. From Oudh.

Variety δ. Obv. legend as stated below.

Coin from Mahanada in Bengal. Obv. legend, *S'rî mahârâjâdhirâja S'rî Kumâra Gupta.* (Proc. A.S.B. 1882, p. 91.)

KUMÂRA GUPTA—*continued.*

Variety ε. 'Kumâra' vertically under king's arm. Obv. marginal legend not read, includes Mahârâja.

S. Obv. marginal legend of about eight illegible characters. Mon. 8*b*.

C. Obv. marginal legend, *Mahârâja*. Obtained at Benares. The king's figure differs in pose from that on the commoner variety.

Variety ζ. Obv. legend as stated below.

Freeling Collection. Obv. legend said by Thomas to be [*de*]*va vijitâvanir avanipati Kumâro Gupto*, as in Fantail Peacock silver coins. Wt. 125. (*Records*, p. 50.) I doubt the genuineness of this coin.

A. Class II. Bowstring outside, and Kumâra vertically outside string.

B.M. I.O. Mon. 10*c*. Wt. 123·5. (Pl. II. Fig. 11.)

B.M. I.O. Mon. 19*b*. Wt. 121·4.

B.M. I.O. Mon. 10*c*. Wt. 119·5.

B. No. 735, 736. Mon. of both 8*b*.

B. No. 719. Mon. illegible. L. hand of goddess raised, no lotus-flower visible.

P.E. pl. xxix. 16. The engraving shows reverse goddess with elbows resting on her knees and both hands turned up. Mon. 8*c*. Rude coin of irregular outline obtained by A.C. at Gayâ. A.C. has now a specimen.

A.A. pl. xviii. 11. Mon. 8*b*. "Very rude coin."

B. Coins of heavy weight, struck apparently to suvarṇa standard, averaging about 146 *grains.*

B.M. R.P.K. Mon. imperfect. Wt. 148·7. (Pl. II. Fig. 12.)

B.M. Yeames. Mon. imperfect. Wt. 143.

B.M. Marsden, mlii. Mon. 8*a*. Wt. 147.

B.M. Marsden, mliii. Mon. imperfect. Wt. 146·5.

B.M. 11 specimens in base metal. Execution very coarse. Wts. 151; 150·6; 150·3; 150·2 (*bis*); 149·2; 147·8; 147·2; 147; 146·8; 146.

A.C. 2 specimens.

Kalîghât hoard. Figured in A.A. pl. xviii. 23. Supposed by Cunningham (Arch. Rep. vol. iii. p. 137) to be a coin of the later Kumâra Gupta of Magadha.

KUMÂRA GUPTA—*continued.*

It is very difficult to arrange satisfactorily these Archer coins of Kumâra Gupta, and I cannot profess to have solved the problem either now, or in my previous publication.

The coins (A) of normal weight (that is to say, of about 125 grains) readily fall into two classes, those with the bow-string inwards, and those with the bow-string outwards. The first class is divided into a number of varieties based on differences in the obverse legend, but this classification is uncertain and unsatisfactory owing to doubts as to what the full legend was. Mr. Sykes' coin and Mr. Carnac's similar specimen (ε) undoubtedly constitute a distinct variety. Both these coins have the bow-string inwards, but have the king's name Kumâra arranged vertically under the arm, as in Class II.

The (ζ) coin in the Freeling collection, mentioned by Thomas, and said to bear the legend *deva vijitâvanir avanipati Kumâro Gupto,* if genuine, is also quite distinct from all other known pieces. But I cannot help feeling doubts about the genuineness of this coin. It is very odd that it should have the legend of the Fantail Peacock silver coins. However, it may be genuine, and it must, for the present, be classed separately. I have not been able to obtain access to the collection of the late Mr. Freeling.

The remaining coins of Class I. seem always to have *Ku* under the king's arm, and the obv. marginal legends noted are as follows:

1. *a. Jayati Mahendra,* with other legend illegible.
2. *β. Parama râjâdhirâja S'rî* [*Kumâra Gupta Mahen*]*dra.*
3. *γ. jatara* (? = [*a*]*jita râ*[*jâ*]*.*
4. *δ. S'rî mahârâjâdhirâja S'rî Kumâra Gupta.*

The *jatara* fragment of legend cannot apparently be reconciled with any of the other inscriptions. The Koṭwâ coin shows that the syllables *Ku* and *râ* were associated with the words *jayati Mahendra,* and these words might very well have formed the conclusion of the third form of legend. The second form of legend appears to be distinct.

KUMÂRA GUPTA—*continued.*

Kumâra Gupta issued silver coins with the title *râjâdhirâja*, and others with the higher title *mahârâjâdhirâja*.

The B heavy coins vary in weight from 143 to 151 grains, and were certainly not struck to the same standard as the coins of normal weight. I formerly placed these pieces, with all those of similar weight, in a supplement, but am now disposed to think that many of these pieces were struck by the kings of the Early or Imperial dynasty. They vary very considerably in style and execution. Some, including the one figured in Pl. II. 12, are not visibly inferior in quality of metal to many of the undoubted coins of the Early dynasty, nor can the design and execution be confidently stated to be ruder. Others are composed of utterly base metal, and are very roughly designed and struck. I formerly misread the reverse legend as *S'rî Mahendraḥ*, which it certainly is not. It is *Srî Kumâra Gupta.* The word Kumâra is plain on some of the base metal coins, and the first syllable of Gupta can be read on the coin figured.

Sir A. Cunningham assigns the Kâlîghât specimen to the Kumâra Gupta of Magadha, who lived about a century later than his namesake, the father of Skanda Gupta. It is probable enough that the base metal specimens belong to his reign, but I now think it most probable that the coins in tolerable gold, like the one figured, belong to the Early Kumâra Gupta, and I would assign the similar coins of Chandra Vikramâditya and Skanda Kramâditya also to the princes of the Early or Imperial dynasty.

The Class II. coins of normal weight, which have the bow-string outwards, are as rude in style and execution as the heavy coins, but undoubtedly bear both the names Kumâra and Mahendra, and there appears to be no reason to doubt that these coins were struck by the Early Kumâra Gupta.

The detached letters which are found, sometimes between the king's feet, and sometimes before his face, on many coins of the Archer type, may be only parts of the marginal

KUMÂRA GUPTA—*continued.*

legend. The character before the king's face is, I think, always part of the legend, but that between his legs may be a mint-mark, or other special sign.

Sir A. Cunningham notes (Arch. Rep. vol. xvi. p. 81) that he has two gold coins of Kumâra with the title Kramâditya, which was specially affected by Skanda Gupta.

Horseman to Right Type.

Obv. King, bareheaded, with curly hair, on high-stepping horse, proceeding to r. No weapon visible, except, perhaps, in one coin. Marginal legend various, and not fully deciphered. One form may be probably restored as **अजित विक्रम महेन्द्र गुप्त देवजनित चितिपति राजति विजय कुमार**, *ajita vikrama Mahendra Gupta devajanita kshitipati râjati vijaya Kumâra,* 'the invincible in might, Mahendra Gupta, begotten of Deva (or 'of the Devas'), the lord of earth, the victorious Kumâra, rules.'

Another form is **परम भागवत महाराजाधिराज श्री महेन्द्र गुप्तः**, *parama bhâgavata mahârâjâdhirâja S'rî Mahendra Guptaḥ,* 'the most devout worshipper of the holy one, the sovereign of Mahârâjas, S'rî Mahendra Gupta.'

Other variations are noted below.

Rev. Goddess seated to l. on Indian wicker-stool (*Morhâ*), and in

(Variety α) holding fillet in r. hand, and lotus-flower in l. hand behind her back;

(Variety β) holding lotus-flower in r. hand, and with l. hand resting on her hip;

(Variety γ) offering fruit (apparently plantains) to a peacock with r. hand, and holding lotus-flower in her l.

Legend of all varieties **अजितो महेन्द्रः**, *ajito Mahendraḥ,* 'unconquered Mahendra.'

Mon. generally wanting.

References and Remarks.—Variety α. Reverse goddess sitting upright, holding fillet in r., and flower in l. hand.

B.M. Bush. Obv. legend seems to include *deva.* Wt. 127·2. (Pl. II. Fig. 13.)

KUMÂRA GUPTA—*continued.*

B.M. E.T. Worn, in poor condition. Wt. 117·3.

B.M. I.O. No. 3. Obv. legend includes *Gupta devajanita kshiti-*.

B. No. 712. Obv. marginal legend illegible.

Koṭwâ hoard. Three specimens, obverse legends of all illegible.

Bharsar hoard. Two specimens. Wts. 124·5 and 125. Much worn. (J.A.S.B. vol. xxi. pp. 398, 400, pl. xii. 8.)

P.E. pl. xxiii. 29. From Lieut. Burt's collection.

P.E. pl. xxx. 4. On obv. margin *-ta vi-* legible.

Hûglî hoard. Obv. legend, as read by Dr. Hoernlé, *Parama bhâgavata . . . . . adhirâja Guptaḥ.* Mon. 8*b*. This is the only instance where a mon. has been observed in this type.

A.A. xviii. 16. Obv. legend includes *Gupta devajanita.* (Records, p. 23 note.)

C. "No. 6. This is a gold coin belonging to Mr. H. Rivett-Carnac. Its find-place is not specified further than 'somewhere between Benares and Fyzabad.' It is a coin of Kumâra Gupta, of the 'Horseman to left' type, (see *ibid.* p. 193) (*sic.* the horseman is to right). I publish it because it has the obverse legend exceptionally well preserved, and may help to establish its correct reading. (See Pl. V. Fig. 5.) It runs thus: + + महरजपत behind the king's back, the vowel marks being clipped off; चि between the king's and the horse's head; तिपति रथीपाद + + + in front and below the horse; there would be space for about six more letters behind the horse, joining the two preserved portions of the legend, though possibly the whole of the space was not occupied by letters. I would suggest to restore the legend thus: महाराजपति-चितिपति-रथीपाद [विजय-कुमारगुप्तः], *mahárájapati—kshitipati—rathîpáda—vijaya—Kumára—Guptaḥ, i.e.* 'the lord of Mahárájas, the lord of the earth, the famous chariot-man, the victorious Kumára Gupta.' The reading of the preserved portion of the legend, as above given, is practically certain, except the *akshara* थी *thí*, the consonant of which is too blurred to be recognizable, and the vowel might be a long *á*. The bracketed portion of the reading I have supplied from another specimen of the 'Horseman to left' type in the Society's collection (see Proceedings A. S. B. for 1882, pp. 111—114, also J.A.S.B., vol. liii. p. 194). The reverse has, as usual, the legend अजितमहेन्द्र *ajita-*

KUMÂRA GUPTA—*continued.*

Mahendra, *i.e.* 'the unconquered Mahendra,' and a female figure seated on a *moṛhá*, holding a fillet in her r., and a long-stalked lotus in her l. hand. There is no mon. The weight is 123·75 grains."—Proc. A.S.B. for 1888, pl. v. 6.[1]

Variety β. Reverse goddess stooping, holding in r. hand an open flower, stalk of which springs from an uncertain object; her l. hand rests on hip.

B. No. 731. King seems to carry a ? bow or quiver on l. side. Obv. legend includes *-jata* or *-jita*, and *pṛithi . . t*, so the word *pṛithivî* 'earth,' evidently formed part of the legend.

Seems to be Tregear's coin figured in P.E. pl. xxx. 3.

E.C.B. Obv. legend illegible. Wt. 126·5.

Variety γ.—Reverse goddess feeding peacock with r. hand, holding lotus-flower in l.

B.M. Prinsep. Obv. legend comprises *-ta Mahendra Gupta*, and eight or nine other characters. Wt. 124·5. Worn. Given to Prinsep by Miss Watson. Figured in P.E. pl. xxiii. 30.

Koṭwâ hoard. Two specimens, with exactly the same obv. legend as above.

B.M. Marsden, mlix. As above. Obv. legend includes *Mahendra Gupta*, followed by ? *bhûpati*. Wt. 125·5. P.E. pl. xxx. 5 much resembles this coin.

B.M. Eden. Obv. legend includes *vijaya kshitipati ra-*. Wt. 124·8.

B.M. Yeames, 1. Wt. 126·7.

B.M. Yeames, 2. Obv. legend includes *mâ* (or *pâ*) *Kshitipati r-*. Wt. 124·7.

B.M. In obv. legend *Gu* legible. Wt. 125·9.

B.M. I.O. No. 1. Obv. legend includes *-gu kshiti-*. Wt. 124.

B.M. I.O. No. 2. Obv. legend includes *kshiti*. Wt. 125·8.

B. No. 734.

Hûglî hoard. One specimen. Obv. legend, as read by Dr. Hoernlé, *Parama bhâgavata . . . S'rî Ma[hendra Gu]pta*. Cf. variety *a*.

[1] The above extract gives Dr. Hoernlé's account of the coin. The collotype figure is too indistinct to allow of the obv. legend being read, but I do not accept the reading *rathîpâda*.

KUMÂRA GUPTA—*continued.*

H. From place in Goṇḍâ District opposite Ajodhya. Obv. legend *ajita Mahendra Gupta.*

A.S.B. Obv. legend *S'rî mahârâjâdhirâja.* It is doubtful to which variety this coin belongs.

A.G. Obv. legend includes *vi . . . pati rajati vij*[*aya*] *Ku-*, and ?*ksh.* Worn. From Oudh.

My previously published account of this type was, I regret to find, inaccurate in several particulars. The errors have now been corrected. The characters which are found on some coins above the horse's head, or between his legs, are parts of the marginal legend. That legend varies much, as already shown. The title *kshitipati,* which occurs, in one form of the legend, is now met with for the first time. One coin seems to give the synonym *bhûpati.* The Horseman to Left coins have legends containing the same titles. The second form of legend *Parama bhâgavata*, etc., is borrowed from the Horseman coins of Chandra Gupta II.

HORSEMAN TO LEFT TYPE.

Obv. King bareheaded, with curly hair, and with bow slung behind his back, on high-stepping horse proceeding to right.

Marginal legend not fully deciphered. It includes **विजित जयति गुप्त चप्र म**, *vijita jayati kshapra ma*, in three instances, and [**महाराजा**] **धिराज क्षितिपति राजति विजय कुमार गुप्त**, [*mahârâjâ*]*dhirâja kshitipati râjati vijaya Kumâra Gupta*, 'the sovereign of Mahârâjas, lord of earth, the victorious Kumâra Gupta rules,' in other cases. In the first form of the legend the meaningless '*kshapra ma*' should perhaps be read '*kshatrapa*.'

Rev. Goddess facing l., seated on Indian wicker stool (*moṛhâ*), with r. hand feeding peacock, and with l. hand holding flower behind her back.

Legend **अजितो महेन्द्रः**, *ajito Mahendraḥ*, 'the unconquered Mahendra.'

No mon.

KUMÂRA GUPTA—*continued.*

References and Remarks.

B.M. No. 1. Wt. 126. Obv. legend **वजत जयत गुप्त चप्र मल च**, *vijita jayati Gupta kshapra mala cha.* (Pl. II. Fig. 14.)

B.M. No. 2. Wt. 123·8 Same obv. legend with the addition of **महन्द्र कम**, *Mahendra Kum—*, the letters *hendra* not being quite certain. The character on both these coins which I have rendered *l* looks like that letter, but ought apparently to be an *h*. The legend of No. 2 is blundered, as if the die had slipped.

B.M. No. 3. Enniskillen. Wt. 123·2. Obv. legend illegible.

B. No. 733. Obv. legend illegible.

Koṭwâ hoard. One poor specimen.

Bharsar hoard. No. 1 of Mahendra. Wt. 124. Obv. legend read by Kittoe as *Mahendra Kumâra.*

Bharsar hoard. No. 2. Ditto, but obv. legend illegible. Wt. 124. (J.A.S.B. vol. xxi. p. 399.)

Hûglî hoard. One specimen. Obv. legend, as read by Dr. Hoernlé, *Gupta kshapra mahâ . . ma . . . vijita jayati.* Cf. B.M. Nos. 1 and 2.

A.S.B. No. 1. Obv. legend **धिराज क्षितिपति राजति विजय कुमार [गुप्त]**, *-dhirâjakshitipati râjati vijaya Kumâra* [*Gupta*], as read by Dr. Hoernlé. From Midnapur District, Bengal.

A.S.B. No. 2. Apparently similar.

A.C. Three specimens.

Coin in Freeling Collection, cited in Thomas' Revised Catalogue, and a coin belonging to Mrs. White of Fatehgarh, engraved in **As. Res. vol. xvii. pl. i. 18.**

The legends seem identical or nearly so with those of the first form of the Horseman to Right coins of the same king, but require elucidation. The word *kshapra* which is read on some coins is meaningless, and the reading requires correction. A silver forgery of this type, obtained apparently at Kanauj, was exhibited in April, 1887, when Dr. Hoernlé observed that it was known that forgeries of the kind were carried on at Kanauj.—(Proc. A.S.B. 1887, p. 124.)

KUMÂRA GUPTA—*continued.*

Peacock Type.

Obv. King bareheaded, with curly hair, standing to l., and with r. hand offering fruit (seemingly a bunch of plantains) to a peacock, which stands facing r.

In variety *a* the king stands upright, and the peacock's neck is extended full-length.

In variety *β* the king is stooping, and the peacock's neck is not fully extended.

Marginal legend of not less than fourteen characters. It certainly includes the word *jayati*, 'is victorious,' and seems to include the name *Kumâra.*

Rev. Goddess, probably Kumârî Devî, riding a peacock, holding a mace or sceptre (? lotus bud) in l. hand, and sometimes, apparently, a fillet in r. hand, which is usually empty.

In variety *a* peacock and goddess turned to l., with altar in front of peacock.

In variety *β* peacock and goddess face front, as in the Fantail Peacock silver coins. No altar.

Legend **महेन्द्र कुमारः**, *Mahendra Kumârah.* No mon.

References and Remarks.—Variety a. King upright. Rev. peacock in profile, with altar.

B.M. Lind. Wt. 128·4. Finely executed. (Pl. III. Fig. 1.)
B.M. Nathan. Wt. 126·5.
E.C.B. No. 3. From Jhûsî hoard. Wt. 128·6.
C. Wt. 127·6 From Allâhâbâd.
A.C. One specimen, from Allâhâbâd.
A.S.B. One specimen.
W.T. One specimen.
Swiney collection. A.A. pl. xviii. 13.

Variety β. King stooping. Rev. peacock and goddess facing front. No altar.

B.M. I.O. Wt. 126. (Pl. III. Fig. 2.)
E.C.B. No. 1. Wt. 128·2.
E.C.B. No. 2. Wt. 127·8. Both these coins from Jhûsî hoard. *Jayati* legible on obv.
A.C. One specimen, found at or near Allâhâbâd.

KUMÂRA GUPTA—*continued.*

C. One specimen, obtained at Benares. Wt. 127·5.

A.G. Wt. 127·6. From Oudh.

A.S.B. One specimen.

Bharsar hoard. No. 3 of Kumâra. Rev. goddess holds fillet and sceptre. Kittoe doubtfully read *S'rî Kumâra* on obv., and *S'rîmad Kumâra* on rev., but the correct rev. reading is *Mahendra Kumâraḥ*. Wt. 124. (J.A.S.B. vol. xxi. p. 397, pl. xii. 7.)

Koṭwâ hoard. Two specimens. *Jayati* legible on obv. of one.

There is no doubt that this Peacock type belongs to the reign of Kumâra Gupta. The reverse legend *Mahendra Kumâra* can be made out on several coins. The peacock was the special emblem of Kumâra Gupta.

The obverse legend cannot be fully deciphered on any coin I know of. The only certain word in it is *jayati*, and the name *Kumâra* is almost certain.

The mechanical execution of the Lind coin in the B.M. is unusually delicate, and the photograph does not do it justice.

I cannot discover any indication to show whether this type was struck early or late in the reign. Specimens of it seem chiefly to come from the finds at or near Allâhâbâd, but they are not confined to that locality.

LION-TRAMPLER TYPE.

Obv. King standing to r., bareheaded, wearing waistcloth; in energetic attitude, with bow in l. hand, and with l. foot trampling on body of lion, which is falling backwards.

The obv. legend includes words which read as श्री सिच (or सैच) देवत, *S'rî Siksha* (or *Saiksha*) *devata.*

Rev. Goddess, facing front, seated on lion, which is usually turned to r.

In variety *a* she holds fillet in r. hand, while her l. hand rests empty on her hip, or holds cornucopiæ.

In variety *β* her r. hand is extended open, and empty, while her l. hand is raised above her shoulder, holding lotus-flower.

Legend, apparently in both varieties, श्री महेन्द्र सिङ्ह, *S'rî Mahendra Siṅha.*

Mon.

KUMÂRA GUPTA—*continued.*

References and Remarks.

Koṭwâ hoard. Obv. legend reads सिचे द्वेवत, *S'rî Sikshe devata.* Rev. Lion to r., legend complete. Mon. 8*a*.

Boys. Similar coin, with same mon. In the rev. legend the vowel mark is placed by mistake over the *m* instead of the *h*. Obv. legend श्री सैच द्वेवत, *S'rî Saiksha devata.* The vowel mark over the *S* is double (‹‹), and there is a dot between the *S* and the *ksh*, so that the word may be read *Saiṇksha.* The characters जयत्य ति, *jayatya ti* seem to precede *S'rî.*

Hûglî hoard. One specimen. Rev. legend complete.

Tregear collection. Obv. legend, as read by Prinsep, -त महेन्द्र जय श्री, *-ta Mahendra jaya S'rî.* Mon. 8*a*. Figured in P.E. pl. xxx. 8. Obtained at Jaunpur. The engraving shows a cornucopiæ in l. hand of rev. goddess. Lion to r.

Variety β. Rev. goddess with r. hand extended open and empty, and l. hand raised, holding lotus-flower.

A.G. Obv. legend illegible. Rev. legend incomplete. Mon. 8*b*. Wt. 127·2

W.T. One specimen.

The obv. legend is very puzzling; the characters on the Koṭwâ and Boys coins are distinct. The title *Mahendra* shows that this rare type must be assigned to Kumâra Gupta. Two coins in **A.S.B.** cabinet seem to belong to this type, and in one of them the rev. lion faces l.

COMBATANT LION TYPE.

Obv. King standing, facing nearly full front, wearing cap and Indian waistcloth, with his l. hand raised to his shoulder. In his r. hand he holds bow, having discharged arrow into mouth of attacking lion, the forepart of which is shown on l. margin.

Under king's left arm कु *Ku.*

Marginal legend includes श्री महेन्द्र सिङ्ह पराक्रमः, *S'rî Mahendra siṅha parâkramaḥ,* 'S'rî Mahendra with the might of a lion.'

KUMÂRA GUPTA—*continued.*

Rev. Goddess (probably Kumârî Devî) standing, slightly stooping to l. holding lotus-flower in her l. hand, and with r. hand offering fruit to a standing peacock, which faces r.

Marginal legend कुमार गुप्ताधिराज, *Kumâra Guptâdhirâja.*

Mon.

References and Remarks.

B.M. I.O. Mon. 8*a*. Wt. 126·1. The obv. legend includes मत्य, and क्र or कु, *matya,* and *kra* or *ku.* (Pl. III. 3.)

A.C.

Bharsar hoard. No. 1 of Kumâra Gupta. Obv. legend illegible. Mon. 8*a*. Wt. 124·5. (J.A.S.B. vol. xxi. p. 397.)

S. "One Kumâra Gupta, belonging to Mr. Sykes, of the 'Combatant lion' type (as *ibid.* p. 197, pl. iv. fig. 3), weight 119·75 grains; the obverse legend is very imperfect; on left margin there are traces of three letters, the last two of which look like क्रम *krama* (perhaps विक्रम *vikrama*); on the right margin there are traces of seven letters, the first two looking like द्य श्री *dya śri,* and the last like कु *ku*; there must have been other letters below the king and behind the lion, joining the two preserved portions, and making up कुमारगुप्तस्य *Kumâra Guptasya,* the initial कु *ku* of which is preserved. The reverse legend reads clearly कुमारगुप्ताधिराज्ञो, *Kumâra Guptâdhirâjño* (not merely *Kumâra Guptâdhirâja*)." [1]

P.E. pl. xxiii. 28. Collected by Cunningham at Benares. Mon. 8*a*.

Swiney collection. Similar coin, noticed in A.A. p. 423.

A.S.B. Exhibited coin. Obv. legend read as beginning with *S'rî mâ-*, a second *S'rî* on r. margin. (Proc. A.S.B. 1881.)

A very rare type. The reading of the obv. legend, so far as it has been deciphered, rests mainly on the following observations of Sir A. Cunningham:

"Ancient coins are occasionally found at Mahâsthân [in the Bogra or Bâgraha District, Lower Bengal],[2] and its suburbs. About 1862 a number of gold coins were found at Bâhmanpâra,

[1] Dr. Hoernlé in Proc. A.S.B. for 1888. The references are to my Catalogue of Gupta Gold Coins.

[2] Identified with Paundra Vardhana, a city mentioned by Hiuen Tsiang, the capital of the country known as Paundra des'a, or Varendra, or Eastern Gauḍa, supposed to be the region called Mahâ Kântâra in the Allâhâbâd Pillar Gupta inscription. (Arch. Rep. vol. xv. pp. 102-112.)

KUMÂRA GUPTA—*continued.*

out of which Mr. Beveridge obtained two. . . . They were both Gupta coins, one of Chandra Gupta II., and the other of Kumâra Gupta. . . . I am able to give a more complete reading of the legends on both sides [*scil.* of the latter] from a coin in my own collection. *Obv.* S'rî Mahendra Siṅha parâkrama. *Rev.* Kumâra Gupta. . ."—(Arch. Rep. vol. xv. p 116.)

The reverse legend with the title *adhirâja* is plain on more than one specimen. The obv. legend is remarkable for the use of the word *parâkrama*, which was specially affected by Samudra Gupta. Prinsep had succeeded in deciphering the word on the coin he figured.

Two Queens Type.

Obv. King standing to front in centre of field, with both hands clasped on his breast, apparently clad in a long robe. On each side a standing female, with one hand raised towards the central figure, and the other resting on her hip. The central figure is the shortest. Above the king's r. shoulder the bird standard. To the r. of the king **कुमार**, *Kumâra*, and to the l. **गुप्त**, *Gupta*. The letters lie on their side; the word *Kumâra* is read from above, and the word *Gupta* from below.

Marginal legend of about thirty characters all round the coin, quite illegible.

Rev. Goddess to the front, seated on lotus, from l. corner of which two leaf or flower-buds spring. In her r. hand she holds a bud, and her l. rests empty on her hip.

Legend on r. margin **श्री प्रतापः**, *S'rî Pratâpaḥ*. Mon.

References and Remarks.

B.M. Presented by Mr. H. Rivett-Carnac, C.I.E., who bought the coin at Mathurâ. Mon. 8*b*. Wt. 115. (Pl. III. Fig. 4.) This very peculiar piece is at present unique, but there is no reason to doubt its genuineness. A notice of it, with a poor woodcut, was published in Proc. A.S.B. Nov. 1883, p. 144. The legend shows that the obv. central figure is the king, and I think the females must certainly be his consorts. The buds springing from the reverse lotus are noticeable, and the title *S'rî Pratâpa* has not been met with elsewhere.

KUMÂRA GUPTA—*continued.*

Aśwamedha Type.

Obv. Thick-barrelled horse, with breast band, standing to r., occupying field, and facing a pole carrying pennons, which float over the horse.

Marginal legend illegible.

Rev. Female standing to l., facing a standard with vase-shaped head, and adorned with pennons. She carries a yak's tail fly-whisk (*chauṛi*) in her r. hand, resting on her shoulder; her l. hand hangs down, and seems to hold a small object.

Legend following r. margin श्री अश्वमेध महेन्द्र, *S'rî aśwamedha mahendra.* No mon.

References and Remarks.

A.C. At present unique; obtained at Mathurâ. Wt. 124·5. (Pl. III. Fig. 5.) The *obv.* and *rev.* devices closely resemble those of the Aśwamedha medals of Samudra Gupta, the most striking difference being that the horse in this coin is turned to the r.

The legend on the Aśwamedha pieces of Samudra Gupta is *aśwamedha parâkrama*—here it is clearly *S'rî aśwamedha mahendra.* Mahendra was the special personal title of Kumâra Gupta, and, so far as is known at present, was not assumed by any other member of the dynasty. The legend therefore indicates that this new type must be assigned to Kumâra Gupta. The style of the reverse female figure leads to the same conclusion. She has the stumpy bent figure which is characteristic of Kumâra's coins, and is quite different from the tall, upright figures of the standing females on Samudra's coinage. This coin is the only evidence that Kumâra Gupta performed the *aśwamedha* sacrifice. There is nothing to show whether the coin was struck early or late in his reign.

SKANDA GUPTA.

King and Queen Type.

Obv. Bird-standard, with pennons, in centre of field; king bare-headed, with curly hair, standing in l. field, facing r.;

SKANDA GUPTA—*continued.*

queen standing in r. field opposite king. King wears either a waistcloth (*dhotî*), or short drawers (*janghiyâ*), and armlets, and with l. hand grasps middle of bow, the string of which is parallel and next to standard. His r. hand rests on his hip. Queen wears Indian woman's waistcloth (*lahangâ*), and in r. hand holds up to the bird-standard an object, probably a flower.

Marginal legend quite illegible, but it probably included the names of both king and queen.

Rev. Goddess (Lakshmî) seated cross-legged on lotus-flower seat, holding lotus-flower in l., and fillet in r. hand.

Legend on r. margin श्री स्कन्द गुप्तः, *S'rî Skanda Guptaḥ.* Mon.

References and Remarks.

B.M. **Prinsep.** Mon. 3*a*. Wt. 128·8. (Pl. III. Fig. 6.) This coin was purchased at Kanauj by Mr. Bacon, who presented it to Prinsep. It has been engraved in P.E. pl. xxiii. 24, and As. Res. vol. xvii. pl. i. 12.

A.S.B. One specimen.

This type is one of the rarest in the Gupta series. I have never heard of any specimen except the two above mentioned. The analogy of the King and Queen coins of Chandra Gupta I. makes it almost certain that the figures on the obverse are those of Skanda Gupta and his queen. Her name is not mentioned in the extant inscriptions. The Two Queens type of Kumâra Gupta may also be compared.

ARCHER TYPE.

Obv. King with curly hair, wearing tailed coat, standing upright to l., holding arrow in r. hand, which is extended across the bird-standard adorned with pennons, and in l. hand holding bow, the string of which is turned inwards.

Under king's l. arm स्कन्द, *Skanda,* arranged vertically. In Class B. a crescent above name.

Marginal legend not deciphered. In Class B. it includes *parama vi . . . deva S'rî.*

SKANDA GUPTA—*continued.*

Rev. Goddess (Lakshmî), as usual, seated cross-legged on lotus-flower, holding fillet in r., and lotus-flower in l. hand.

Legend **श्री स्कन्द गुप्तः**, *S'rî Skanda Guptaḥ*, in Class A., and **क्रमादित्यः**, *Kramâdityaḥ*, 'the sun of power,' in Class B.

References and Remarks.—Class A. Coins of normal (stater) weight, averaging about 129 *grains.*

B.M. I.O. No. 2. Mon. 8*a*. Wt. 132·5. (Pl. III. Fig. 7.)

B.M. I.O. No. 1. Mon. imperfect. Wt. 129·5.

B.M. Brind. Mon. 3*b*. Wt. 130·1.

Bharsar hoard. 6 specimens, viz. No. 1, mon. 3*b*, wt. 129·25, and two duplicates, wt. 125 each; No. 2, mon. 3*b* or 4*c*, wt. 129·25; No. 3, mon. as No. 2, wt. of two specimens 130 each.—(J.A.S.B. vol. xxi. pp. 398–400.)

A.G. Mon. 3*a*. Wt. 132·3. From Oudh.

Coin from Mahanada. (Proc. A.S.B. May 1882, p. 91.)

P.E. pl. xxix. 18. From Cunningham's collection. Dug up eight miles from Ghâzîpur in Ghâzîpur District, N.W.P. Mon. 3*a*.

P.E. pl. xxx. 10. From Tregear collection. Mon 3*a*.

Class B. Heavy coins, apparently struck to suvarṇa standard, averaging 142·3 *grains. Rev. legend 'Kramâdityaḥ.'*

B.M. Prinsep. Mon. imperfect. Wt. 141·4. (Pl. III. Fig. 8.)

M.B. Marsden, mlv. Ditto. Wt., including attached ring, 150.

B.M. Rivett-Carnac. Wt. 141·7 and 142.

B. No. 684. Mon. 8*b*.

B. No. 727. Agrees with P.E. pl. xxix. 17. Obv. legend of eight characters, beginning **परम विक्र** [or **क**] **र**, *parama vikra* [*or ka*] *ra*.

B. No. 728. A peculiar character before king's face. Mon. 8*a*.

B. No. 730. Agrees with P.E. pl. xxiii. 22. Obv. marginal legend **त देव श्री**, *ta deva S'rî.*

A.C. Two specimens. One was obtained at Gayâ.

P.E. pl. xxiii. 20. A rude coin.

Mr. Rivett-Carnac, at the beginning of 1887, showed me fifteen of the Kramâditya coins. Fourteen of these were of the usual size, about ·8 in diameter, the fifteenth was a larger

SKANDA GUPTA—*continued.*

and flatter coin, nearly a full inch in diameter. Two of the fourteen are now in the B.M. One was obtained at Bhitarî, an ancient site in the Ghâzîpur District, N.W.P., where there are remains of buildings of the time of Kumâra Gupta, and a well-known inscription of the reign of Skanda Gupta. The other coins were, I think, obtained at or near Benares.

I formerly relegated the Kramâditya pieces to a supplement, and doubted if they were issued by Skanda Gupta. But, on reconsideration, I do not find any sufficient reason for supposing that they were struck by any other prince. No Skanda Kramâditya is known except he be the Skanda Gupta, son of Kumâra Gupta, and numerous silver coins of Skanda Gupta Kramâditya exist. The crescent under the king's arm occurs on coins which undoubtedly belong to Kumâra Gupta of the Early or Imperial dynasty. The difference in style between the heavy and the normal weight Archer coins of Skanda is not sufficient to warrant the assignment to them of different dates. I now believe that Chandra Gupta II., Kumâra Gupta, and Skanda Gupta all, for some reason unknown, struck gold coins, both according to the Greek stater (*aureus*) standard, and the native *suvarṇa* standard.

The reverse legend of the normal weight Archer coins of Skanda is the same as that of his King and Queen coins.

SUPPLEMENT.

The princes named Nara Bâlâditya, Prakâśâditya, and ? Vîra Sena Kramâditya, whose coins are briefly discussed in the following pages, do not seem to belong to the Imperial Gupta family, at least to its direct line. It is quite possible that they were connected with it by ties of blood.

A strict adherence to my plan would preclude me from noticing these coins, but I do not like to pass them over. The coins of ? Vîra Sena Kramâditya are so remarkable that they deserve a fuller notice than they have yet received, and the present is a convenient opportunity for noticing them.

The coins of Nara Bâlâditya and Prakâśâditya were included in my former catalogue, but my descriptions of them in some points require correction, and the necessary corrections can be made more conveniently now than on any other occasion.

I regret that I am still unable to identify the king who took the title of Prakâśâditya, and, in spite of the rude style of his coins, I should not be surprised if he turned out to be either Kumâra or Skanda Gupta. In the Bharsar hoard his coins were found associated with coins of Samudra Gupta, Chandra Gupta II., Kumâra Gupta, Skanda Gupta, and with those of no one else. We now know that Skanda Gupta certainly assumed the title of Vikramâditya, as well as that of Kramâditya, and that Kumâra Gupta took the style of S'rî Pratâpa, as well as his better-known title of Mahendra. There is thus no *à priori* improbability in the assumption that the title Prakâśâditya may belong to either Kumâra or Skanda Gupta. The difference in style between the Prakâśâditya coins and some issues of Kumâra and Skanda Gupta is not sufficient to warrant any certain inference as to difference of date. The contrast in style between the various issues of Chandra Gupta II. is very great, and, in a less degree, similar variations in execution and design may be perceived in the coinages of Kumâra Gupta and Skanda Gupta.

But it is more likely that Prakâśâditya is a title of an early member of the later dynasty of the Guptas of Magadha, which ruled from about A.D. 480 to A.D. 700 or a little later. The inscriptions do not mention Prakâśâditya, who must not be confounded with Prakaṭâditya, son of Bâlâditya, who seems to have been king of Benares at the close of the seventh century A.D., and is mentioned in the Sârnâth inscription.[1]

The same document mentions an earlier Bâlâditya.

I cannot venture to decide on the identity of Nara Bâlâditya of the coins. Sir A. Cunningham is disposed, he tells me, to identify him with the King Bâlâditya of Magadha, the opponent of the Hûṇa King Mihirakula. Mr.

[1] Corpus Inscr. Ind. vol. iii. No. 79, p. 284.

Fleet fixes A.D. 515 as the date for the commencement of the career of Mihirakula,[1] and Mr. Beal, though making some corrections in Mr. Fleet's detailed arguments, accepts that date.[2] I doubted it at one time, but now admit that it seems to be established. The date of A.D. 520 or A.D. 530 would very well suit the style and epigraphy of the coins of Nara Bâlâditya, but a great obstacle in the way of assigning these coins to the Bâlâditya, the opponent of Mihirakula, is this, that the coins are as much Hindu in character as the coins of Kumâra and Skanda Gupta of the same Archer type, whereas the opponent of Mihirakula "profoundly honoured the law of Buddha."[3] We should expect to see Buddhist symbols on his coins. The name Nara does not seem to occur in the inscriptions.

Nara Bâlâditya may be the father of Prakaṭâditya mentioned in the Sârnâth inscription, and the date thus obtained (*circa* A.D. 650) is a possible one, though rather late for the style of the coins, which look to me a century earlier.

PRAKÂS'ÂDITYA.

Lion and Horseman Type (suvarṇa standard).

Obv. Horseman (king), wearing low cap, advancing to r. to meet a dragon-like animal with open jaws. The horseman carries a bow slung behind him, and in some specimens he seems to be thrusting a weapon into the dragon's mouth, while in others his hand is empty. His body is sometimes upright, sometimes stooped forward.

Some coins show a small bird-standard above the horse's head, another has three dots in the same place, and others have nothing.

Legend behind horseman includes the words देव जयति, *deva jayati*, 'his majesty is victorious.'

Rev. Goddess (Lakshmî), as usual, on lotus-seat, holding fillet in r., and lotus-flower in l. hand.

Legend on r. margin श्री प्रकाशादित्य:, *S'ri Prakâśâdityaḥ*, which means 'the sun of splendour.' Mon.

[1] *Ind. Ant. vol. xv. p. 252.*
[2] *Ibid*, p. 346.
[3] *Ibid.*, p. 246.

PRAKÂŚÂDITYA—*continued.*

References and Remarks.

B.M. R.S. *Obv.*, bird-standard over horse's head. Legend *va ja.* Mon. 10*a*. Wt. 145. (Pl. III. Fig. 9.)

B.M. I.O. No. 1. *Obv.*, three dots over horse's head. Mon. 13. Wt. 145·8. (Pl. III. Fig. 10.)

B.M. Pringle. In bad condition. Wt. 136.

B.M. I O. No. 2. *Obv.*, bird-standard over horse's head, legend *deva jayati.* Mon. imperfect. Wt. 146·2.

A.C. Two specimens. Mon. 8*a*. and 13. Wt. of one 146, and of the other nearly the same.

Bharsar hoard. Nos. 1 and 2. *Obv.*, bird-standard over horse's head. Mon. of both coins 8*a*. Wt. 146 and 145. Gold said to be rich, but the workmanship inferior. (J.A.S.B. vol. xii. p. 400, pl. xii. 9.)

R.A.S. One specimen.

A.A. pl. xviii. 18. Mon. 6.

A.A. pl. xviii. 19. Mon. wanting. From Kanauj.

The obverse device of these coins is compounded of the devices of the Horseman and the Lion types of Chandra Gupta II. and Kumâra Gupta, but is executed in an inferior manner. The figure of the reverse goddess resembles that on the coins of Skanda Kramâditya and Nara Bâlâditya, the crossed legs being drawn as a horizontal bar, without distinguishing one limb from the other. In other respects the execution of these coins is not distinctly inferior to that of the Swordsman coins of Kumâra Gupta, and some of the normal weight Archer coins of the same king, which are very coarsely designed and struck.

Some specimens (Pl. III. Fig. 10) have a character under the horse, which looks like a *u*. A similar character is found on the coins of Vishṇu Chandrâditya, who was probably Vishṇu Gupta Deva of Magadha, who reigned about A.D. 700.[1] But on one of the A.C. coins the character under the horse looks like *r*, and may be part of the marginal legend. Wherever it is not part of the legend, it may be intended for the initial of the king's proper name. Prakâśâditya, like Kramâditya, Vikra-

[1] Arch. Rep vol i. p 40, note; and Corpus Inscr. Ind. vol. iii. p. 217.

PRAKÂŚÂDITYA—*continued.*

mâditya, etc., was doubtless only a title. I do not think that these coins of Prakâśâditya are later than, say, A.D. 550. They look rather earlier than than those of Nara, but it is very difficult to judge the style of semi-barbarous issues. The metal of the Prakâśâditya coins appears to be of better quality than that found in the other *suvarṇa* coinages. Kittoe expressly noted that the gold of the Bharsar coins was rich, and I have not seen any coins of this type in base metal.

NARA BÂLÂDITYA.

ARCHER TYPE (SUVARṆA STANDARD).

Obv. Standing king to l., holding bow in l. and arrow in r. hand. Bird standard as usual. In style the device is much the same as that of the heavy coins of Chandra, Kumâra, and Skanda. Between king's legs ग्रे, *gre*, which does not seem to be part of the marginal legend.

Under king's l. arm नर, *Nara*, arranged vertically.

Marginal legend not deciphered.

Rev. Lakshmî on lotus-seat, holding fillet and flower, in degraded style.

Legend बालादित्य, *Bâlâditya*, 'the young, or rising, sun.' The initial syllable is written वा, *Vâ*. Mon., sometimes omitted, but the omission is probably accidental.

References and Remarks.

B.M. Yeames. Mon. 8*e*. Wt. 148·7. (Pl. III. Fig. 11.)

B.M. Prinsep. Mon. 8*e*. Wt. 144·5.

B.M. A. Newman. Mon. 8*e*. Wt. 143·5.

B. Six specimens.

A.C. Four specimens.

A.G. Mon. 9*a*. Wt. 145·1.

M. mliv. Wt. 146·5. From Kâlîghât hoard.

A.A. pl. xviii. 22. From Kâlîghât hoard. See also Records, p. 24.

Coin from Ranaghat subdivision of Nuddea (Nadiyâ) District. (Proc. A.S.B. 1886, p. 65.)

A.S.B. Some specimens.

W.T. One coin.

The above coins are gold, though the metal is always

NARA BÂLÂDITYA—*continued.*

impure. But a large number of coins bearing the name of Nara are composed of utterly base metal, and are executed with extreme coarseness. Six specimens of this class are in the B.M. collection, and thirty-three similar pieces are in the I.O. collection, now incorporated with the B.M. I did not think it worth while to examine the I.O. base metal coins very minutely, but they do not all bear the name of Nara; many, however, do. As already noted, the B.M. collection includes eleven similar coarse pieces with the name of Kumâra. I am disposed to think that all the coins of this kind are from fifty to two hundred years later than Skanda Gupta, but I cannot profess to assign them definitely. The gold coins of Nara are very much the same in style as the heavy coins in tolerable gold bearing the names of Chandra, Kumâra and Skanda, and are not, I think, far removed from them in date. I do not think it probable that they are later than A.D. 550. The base metal coins look like late imitations of them.

In my former catalogue I erroneously wrote Nâra for Nara, and, following Mr. Thomas, added the cognomen Gupta, for which there is no authority.

VÎRA [? SENA, OR ? SIṄHA] KRAMÂDITYA.

BULL TYPE.

Obv. Standing bull (? cow) to r., with trappings.

Legend above श्री वीर [? सेन or ? सिङ्ह], *S'rî Vîra*[*Sena* or *Siṅha* ?]. Two characters between bull's legs.

Rev. Lakshmî to front on lotus-seat, holding lotus as usual in her l. hand. Her r. hand seems empty, but is cut away. Legend क्रमादित्य, *Kramâditya.* No mon.

Oval, thick coins.

References and Remarks.

B.M. Presented by H. Rivett-Carnac, Esq., C.I.E. Wt. 162·5. (Pl. III. 12.) Noticed in Proc. A.S.B. for 1887, p. 124, pl. i.

The B.M. specimen is one of three coins purchased by Mr. Rivett-Carnac, at or near Benares, I think. Another specimen

VÎRA [? SENA OR ? SIṄHA] KRAMÂDITYA—*continued.*

weighed 169 grains. The coins are oval in form. They seem later than the coins of the Imperial Guptas, though not much later, and are connected with the coinage of Skanda Gupta by the use of the Lakshmî reverse, the bull symbol, and the title Kramâditya. On the coin figured the first three syllables of this title are distinct, and the form of the letter *m* is of the oldest style found on the Gupta coinage. The king's name on the obv. cannot be made out with certainty, but certainly begins with *V* and a vowel mark. The name looks like Vîra Sena. I cannot at present make out to whom the coins belong, or to exactly what period. The weight is very peculiar. The coins may possibly have been struck to the 100 *rati* standard of 182·5 grains, but it is much more probable that they were struck to the standard "called by metrologists the Persian, the standard on which coins were struck in all parts of the Persian Empire, notably the *sigli* stamped with the figure of the Persian king, which must have freely circulated in the northern parts of India, which paid tribute to the Persians. . . . In the Persian standard the unit or drachm weighs 84–86 grains."[1]

These coins of Kramâditya resemble in form the Persian *sigli*, and I have little doubt that they follow the Persian standard of weight, which had been used long before by the Bactrian kings Eukratides, Heliocles, and Antialcidas.

CHAPTER IX.—CATALOGUE OF SILVER COINS.

CONTENTS.

[1] Gardner, The Coins of the Greek and Scythic Kings of Bactria and India in the British Museum, p. lxviii.

CHANDRA GUPTA II.

Vikramâṅka Type.

Obv. Head of king to r., as in the coins of the Satraps of Saurâshṭra, with long hair, moustaches, and collar.

Remains of corrupt Greek letters in front of face. No date.

Rev. Rude representation of a bird (peacock) standing to front, with wings expanded, but tail hidden by the body. A sun or cluster of stars in r. field, sometimes with a crescent.

Marginal legend, without vowel marks above line, श्री गुप्तकुलस्य महाराजाधिराज श्री चन्द्र गुप्त विक्रमाङ्कस्य, *S'rî Guptakulasya mahârâjâdhirâja S'rî Chandra Gupta Vikramâṅkasya*, '[coin] of S'rî Chandra Gupta, sovereign of Mahârâjas, of the S'rî Gupta race.'

References and Remarks.

Freeling. Cluster of stars and minute half-moon in rev. r. upper field. Wt. 31.

First published as unique by Thomas in J.A.S.B. vol. xxiv. p. 503 (1855), and erroneously assigned by him to (S'rî) Gupta, the founder of the Gupta dynasty. Republished by the same author in P.E. vol. ii. p. 94, and in Records, pp. 49–50, with woodcut of rev.

E.C.B. No. 1. Group of stars wanting. Legend incomplete. Title read by E.C.B. as *Vikramârkasya*, but erroneously, the character is *ṅ* not *r*. E.C.B. assigned the coin wrongly to Kumâra Gupta. Received from Dr. Bühler.—(Ind. Ant. vol. vi. pp. 57, 58, with woodcuts, and vol. xiv. p. 65.)

E.C.B. No. 2. Legend as in Freeling coin, the *ṅ* being unmistakeable. Received from Dr. Bühler.—(*Ibid.*)

A.C. No cluster of stars on crescent visible in the lithograph, but the description notes "to the right a sun or star."—(Arch. Rep. vol. ix. p. 23, pl. v. 1.)

The four specimens above described are the only ones at present known to exist. I do not know the exact find-spot of any of them, but Dr. Bühler's coins certainly came from the Bombay Presidency, and I have no doubt that the other specimens also are from the West.

The reading of the legend has been finally settled by Mr. Fleet (Ind. Ant. vol. xiv. p. 65). It is needless to note earlier erroneous readings, or the theories based upon them.

CHANDRA GUPTA II.—*continued.*

Mr. Fleet translates the words *Śrî Guptakulasya* by the phrase 'who belongs to the glorious family of the Guptas,' and Sir A. Cunningham renders them 'the descendant of Srî Gupta.' Either interpretation is legitimate, and I have, therefore, preferred a literal rendering which retains the ambiguity of the original. I think the honorific prefix *Srî* is better left untranslated. No English word has exactly the same connotation.

The reverse device of these coins is certainly a rude diagram of a bird, presumably a peacock, standing to the front, with wings expanded, and tail concealed by the body. It is found also on the coins of Kumâra Gupta and some of those of Skanda Gupta in the same form, and on one class of Skanda Gupta's coinage in a modified, degraded form, which has been called an altar.

The sun, or cluster of stars, and crescent were borrowed from the coinage of the Saurâshṭran Satraps.

I cannot determine whether this type was struck earlier or later than the type next to be described.

Vikramâditya Type.

Obv. As in Vikramâṅka type. The corrupt Greek letters seem to be a corruption of the legend PAO NANO PAO of the Indo-Scythian coins.

Rev. As in Vikramâṅka type, with sun or stars in r. field. Marginal legend, without vowel marks above line, परम भागवत महाराजाधिराज श्री चन्द्र गुप्त विक्रमादित्य, *parama bhâgavata mahârâjâdhirâja S'rî Chandra Gupta Vikramâditya,* 'the most devout worshipper of the holy one, the sovereign of Mahârâjas, S'rî Chandra Gupta Vikramâditya.'

References and Remarks.

B.M. **Bird.**[1] Cluster of six stars in r. upper field of rev. Marginal legend -त महाराज श्री चन्द्र गुप्त व-, *-ta Mahârâja S'rî Chandra Gupta V-*. (Pl. IV. Fig. 1.)

A.C. Two specimens (Arch. Rep. vol. ix. p. 23, pl. v. 2, 3; Ind. Ant. vol. xiv. p. 66).

[1] This coin was erroneously labelled as belonging to Kumâra Gupta.

CHANDRA GUPTA II.—*continued.*

Indian Museum, Calcutta. One specimen found at Sultânganj in Bhâgalpur District, Bengal, along with a coin of Swâmî Rudra Sinha, last Satrap of Saurâshṭra.[1]

Newton. Cluster of seven stars. Found in Kâthiâwâṛ, along with coins of Kumâra Gupta. (J.Bo.Br.R.A.S. vol. vii. p. 11, and fig. 12 of plate; and Records, p. 48.)

E.C.B. See Ind. Ant. vol. vi. p. 57, and vol. xiv. p. 66.

The coins of this type are almost as rare as those of the Vikramâṅka type. The association of the Sultânganj specimen with a coin of the last Satrap of Saurâshṭra is interesting, as supporting the inference justified by other evidence that the conquest of Saurâshṭra was effected by Chandra Gupta II. His inscriptions in Central India must have been recorded when he was on his way to or from his conquests on the western coast. He adopted the Saurâshṭran model for his silver coinage, but with legends to suit his own predilections. The title Vikramâditya is found on his Umbrella gold coins, which I suppose to be the latest of his gold issues, and on one very rare type of his copper coinage. The extreme rarity of both types of the silver coins of Chandra Gupta II. shows that they must have been issued in small numbers, and probably near the close of his reign. The Vaishṇava epithet *paramabhâgavata* occurs on his Horseman gold coins, and on one variety of the Horseman to Right gold coins of Kumâra Gupta, as well as on the silver coins of both Kumâra and Skanda Gupta.

The date 90, in the ancient form, was read by both Sir E. C. Bayley and Mr. Newton on two coins of this type, but Mr. Thomas interpreted the same character as corrupt Greek. Sir E. C. Bayley also wished to read *va* (for *varshe,* 'in the year') *behind* the king's head, but this reading is rejected by Mr. Fleet, who would interpret the character in question as a numeral, either 4 or 5. Mr. Fleet, however, admits that the character *in front* of the king's face, which has been read as 90, is doubtful, and may even be part of a marginal

[1] The discovery of the coin is mentioned in Arch. Rep. vol. x. p. 127. Sir A. Cunningham informs me that it is now in the Indian Museum, Calcutta.

CHANDRA GUPTA II.—*continued.*

pattern. There is no precedent for the engraving of one figure of the legend behind, and another before the king's head, and I do not believe that the coins of this type are dated at all.

No clear reading of a date is to be found on any of the Gupta silver coins, except those with the Fantail Peacock device.

The king's name on the Vikramâditya coins was read by Sir E. C. Bayley and Mr. Newton as Bakra. But this reading is undoubtedly erroneous. The name is Chandra, and nothing else, as correctly read by Sir A. Cunningham and Mr. Fleet. The mistaken reading was due to a slight irregularity in the form of the letters comprising the name on some specimens.

KUMÂRA GUPTA.

Winged Peacock Type.

Obv. Head of king to r., as in coins of Chandra Gupta II. Corrupt Greek letters, sometimes before, and sometimes behind the head. Two crescents on cap.

Rev. Peacock standing to front with wings expanded, but tail concealed, sometimes very rudely executed. Sun or cluster of stars seems to be wanting in variety *a*, but is sometimes present in variety *β*. Legend of variety *a* परम भागवत राजाधिराज श्री कुमार गुप्त महेन्द्रादित्य (or महेन्द्रस्य), *parama bhâgavata râjâdhirâja S'rî Kumâra Gupta Mahendrâditya* (or *Mahendrasya*), 'the most devout worshipper of the holy one, the sovereign of Râjas, S'rî Kumâra Gupta Mahendrâditya,' *or* '[Coin] of the most devout S'rî, etc., Kumâra Gupta Mahendra.'

Legend of variety *β*, as above, with the addition of महा, *mahâ*, 'great,' to the title राजाधिराज, *râjâdhirâja.*

Vowel marks not inserted above the line.

References and Remarks.—Variety a, with title râjâdhirâja.

B.M. Prinsep. One crescent on king's cap, the second being obliterated. Behind head O I O I O (written vertically).

KUMÂRA GUPTA—*continued.*

Rev. legend complete; it appears to end in *-asya*, not *âditya* (Pl. IV. Fig. 2).

B M. Prinsep. Ten other specimens, in some of which the Greek letters are before, and in others behind the head. The legend of two of these ends in *-asya*, not *-âditya*.

B.M. Bird. Two specimens, which may belong to variety *β*.

B M. A. Grant. One specimen, which may belong to variety *β*.

A.C. 24 specimens. (Arch. Rep. vol. ix. p. 24, pl. v. 4; and Ind. Ant. vol. xvi. p. 66).

Variety β, with title mahârâjâdhirâja.

A.C. Four specimens. (Arch. Rep. vol. ix. p. 24, pl. v. 5; and Ind. Ant. vol. xvi. p. 66).

B.M. Steuart. Two specimens, cluster of seven stars.

B.M. Bird. Two specimens, cluster of stars.

B.M. Prinsep. One specimen, no stars.

Mr. Thomas observes that we have multitudes of specimens of this type, that is to say, of both varieties. Out of 65 coins found at Ahmadâbâd in Guzerât, eight belonged to variety *a* (J.Bo.Br.R.A.S. vol. vi. p. xlvii, 1861). A treasure of 1395 coins found at Sanand in the Satâra District of the Bombay Presidency consisted of about 1100 pieces of Kumâra Gupta's Winged Peacock type (variety not stated), and of nearly 300 coins of the kings of Valabhi (*ibid.* pp. li and lxxi). The Thâkur of Bhaunagar in Kâthiâwâṛ sent in nine specimens of variety *a* (J.Bo.Br.R.A.S. vol. viii. p. xiii, 1867).

Thirteen very perfect examples were found at Ellichpur in 1851, and presented to Sir H. M. Elliot. The average weight of these coins was 29 grains, and the highest weight 32 grains, but some specimens of the type weigh 33.

Mr. Newton's coin, a specimen of variety *β*, is supposed to have the date 90, or 90 with a unit, behind the head, the numeral being preceded by a character like an iota, which is commonly found on the coins of the Satraps of Saurâshṭra, and is conjectured to be a mint-mark (J.Bo.Br.R.A.S. vol.

KUMÂRA GUPTA—*continued.*

vii. p. 3, and fig. 12 of plate; Records, p. 7, No. x*, with woodcut of *obv.*). But I very much doubt the correctness of the reading of this solitary date, and suspect that the supposed numeral is only a corrupt Greek letter.

Some specimens of variety *β* sent from Kâthiâwâṛ by Major Watson to Mr. Burgess are described and figured in Records, pp. 44, 45, and figures 11–16 of autotype plate.[1] None of these have any date, nor has any specimen of the type, which I have seen.

Of Mr. Burgess' coins, No. 11 has cluster of stars in lower rev. r. field; Nos. 12 and 14–16 have similar clusters in upper r. field, the stars varying in number. No. 13 is a larger coin than the others, and the king is depicted with a thick neck, and a form of earring different from that on the other coins.

It may reasonably be conjectured that the variety *a* coins with the inferior title *râjâdhirâja* were struck earlier than the variety *β* pieces, and it is possible that Kumâra Gupta struck the former as Viceroy for his father, but there is no independent evidence that he ever was Viceroy. The supposed tradition published by Major Watson is known to be a forgery.

Mr. Fleet reads the concluding word of the legend as *Mahendrâditya*, and this reading is no doubt correct for many coins. But the earlier reading *Mahendrasya* is supported by three coins in the British Museum. The use of the genitive agrees with the form of legend on Chandra Gupta's Vikramâṅka coins. The title *Mahendrâditya* has not yet been met with on the gold coins.

In addition to the references given above, notices of coins of this type will be found in A.A. pl. xv. 17, 18; J.A.S.B. vol. xxiv. p. 505; J.R.A.S. vol. XII. (o.s.) p. 65, Pl. II. 39-42; and P.E. vol. ii. p. 96, pl. xxxvii. 16, 17.

These coins seem to occur only in the Bombay Presidency. The coins figured by Prinsep came from Kachchh.

[1] Mr. Burgess has recently presented these coins to the B.M.

KUMÂRA GUPTA—*continued.*

TRIDENT TYPE.

Obv. King's head to r., as usual, rudely executed. Traces of ? Greek legend.

Rev. Trident (*triśûl*) in centre of field. Star cluster and crescent.

Marginal legend, as read by Mr. Newton, **परम भागवत [राजाधिराज] श्री कुमार गुप्त महेन्द्रस्य**, *parama bhâgavata* [*râjâdhirâja*] *S'rî Kumâra Gupta Mahendrasya*, '[coin] of S'rî Kumâra Mahendra, [sovereign of Râjas], most devout worshipper of the holy one.'

References and Remarks.

Newton. From Kâṭhiâwâṛ (J.Bo.Br R.A.S. vol. vii. p. 10, and fig. 11 of plate).

This type is known only from the coin published by Mr. Newton, and rests on his authority. The trident, as engraved in his plate, is distinct. It is possible that the title ought to be read *Mahendrâditya.* Similar tridents are found on the coins of Senapati Bhaṭârka, and the other princes of Valabhi, who succeeded the Guptas in Kâṭhiâwâṛ (Saurâshṭra).

There are three trident coins in the Bodleian collection, but I did not make out the legends, and the coins probably belong to the Valabhi series.

FANTAIL PEACOCK TYPE.

Obv. King's head to r., as usual, but rather larger than in preceding types. No Greek legend. Date in ancient numerical symbols arranged vertically in front of face.

Rev. Peacock standing to front, with expanded wings, and outspread tail, clearly designed and executed. Sometimes a cluster of stars in lower field.

Marginal legend, with vowel-marks in full, **विजितावनिरवनिपति कुमार गुप्तो देवो** (or **देवं**, or **देव**) **जयति**, *vijitâvaniravanipati Kumâra Gupto devo* (or *devaṃ*, or *deva*) *jayati*, 'victorious is his majesty, the lord of the earth, Kumâra Gupta, who has conquered the earth.'

KUMÂRA GUPTA—*continued.*

References and Remarks.

B.M. **Mayhew.** Date ? 135.

B.M. **Prinsep.** Three specimens in poor condition. The king's name is illegible, but the coins seems to be Kumâra's.

B. At least one specimen.

A.C. Nine specimens (Arch. Rep. vol. ix. p. 24, pl. v. 6, 7; Ind. Ant. vol. xiv. p. 66).

The Fantail Peacock coins, both of Kumâra Gupta and Skanda Gupta, were evidently, like the gold and copper coinages, minted in Northern India. They are tolerably common in the North-Western Provinces, but are rare elsewhere. Sir. A. Cunningham informs me that they are most commonly obtained at Benares, Ajodhya, Mathurâ, and places near those cities. A considerable number have been found near Sahâranpur, and at Bûriyâ on the Jumna. The late Mr. Thomas possessed six specimens of Kumâra's coinage, procured mostly at Kanauj (Records, p. 50, figs. 22, 23 of autotype plate); Colonel Stacy had six, and Mr. Freeling seven, all probably collected within the North-Western Provinces (J.A.S.B. vol. xxiv. p. 512).

The type is also described and illustrated in P.E. vol. i. p. 338, pl. xxvii. 10–12; and J.R.A.S. Vol. XII. (o.s.) Pl. II. It is very poorly represented in the British Museum collection, but I have no doubt that numerous specimens exist in private cabinets.

The Greek legend is altogether wanting in all the coins with this Fantail Peacock device. The peacock is represented much in the same way as in variety β of Kumâra Gupta's gold Peacock coins. The device on the silver coins of Skanda Gupta, Budha Gupta, Bhîmasena, Toramâṇa, and Iśâna Varman (Arch. Rep. vol. ix. pp. 25–27), is a repetition of that on the silver coins of Kumâra Gupta, and the reverse legend on all these coins also is substantially the same.

The weight of the best-preserved specimens is between 35 and 36 grains, but ordinary specimens weigh about 30 grains.

KUMÂRA GUPTA—*continued.*

The dates are recorded in the ancient Indian notation, which employed separate symbols for each of the hundreds, tens, and units, the meaning of which was independent of position. But on the coins the symbol for 100 is always placed first, then the symbol for the decade, and then the unit, and they are arranged vertically thus, $\begin{smallmatrix}100\\40\\4\end{smallmatrix} = 144$. The forms of the numerals do not agree exactly with those used on stone and copper inscriptions, or on the coins of the Satraps of Saurâshṭra, but the symbols on the Gupta coins can be read by the aid of Pandit Bhagvanlâl Indrajî's table in Ind. Ant. vol. vi. p. 42.

The dates refer to the so-called Gupta era, of which the year 1 corresponded to A.D. 320–21, old style.

The dates hitherto recognized on the coins of Kumâra Gupta are 121, 124, 128, 129, and 130. The Mayhew coin in the B.M. seems to me to be dated in 135, and a coin from the Prinsep collection, wt. 35·8 (Fig. 56 of Pl. II. J.R.A.S. Vol. XII. O.S.), seems to bear the same date.

SKANDA GUPTA.

WINGED PEACOCK TYPE.

Obv. Head of king to r., as usual, but rudely executed. Two crescents on cap. Remains of corrupt Greek legend either before king's face, or at back of his head. No date.

Rev. Device in a few coins is the same as that of the Winged Peacock coins of Kumâra Gupta, and is plainly a bird. Much more commonly it is a rude diagram, which is probably intended for the outline of a bird standing on a pedestal, but is so obscure that it has been called an altar.

Marginal legend, vowel marks above line being omitted;

Variety α.—परम भागवत महाराजाधिराज श्री स्कन्द गुप्त क्रमादित्य, *parama bhâgavata mahârâjâdhirâja S'rî Skanda Gupta Kramâditya*, 'the most devout worshipper of the holy one, sovereign of Mahârâjas, S'rî Skanda Gupta Kramâditya.'

Variety β.—As above, substituting विक्रमादित्य, *Vikramâditya*, for क्रमादित्य, *Kramâditya*, and omitting *mahârâjâdhirâja.*

Variety γ.—As above, substituting परमादित्य, *paramâditya*, for क्रमादित्य, *Kramâditya.*

SKANDA GUPTA—*continued.*

References and Remarks.—Variety a. With title Kramâditya.

B.M. **Prinsep.** More than sixty specimens. A few of these (at the end of tray No. 3) have a fairly distinct peacock, as on the coins of Kumâra Gupta. The rest (comprising the fifty-one pieces in tray No. 2, and part of tray No. 3) have the corrupt device, which Thomas calls an altar. (Pl. IV. 7.)

A.C. (Arch. Rep. vol. ix. p. 25, pl. v. 11, and Ind. Ant. vol. xiv. p. 67.)

Variety β.—With title Vikramâditya.

B.M. Ten specimens in tray No. 3. (Pl. IV. 6.)

Variety γ.—With title Paramâditya.

B.M. The last two coins in tray No. 3.

This type is also described in J.R.A.S. Vol. XII. o.s. pp. 65, 67, Pl. II. 43, 44, 49–51, all three varieties; J.A.S.B. vol. vii. pl. xii. 18–21; J.A.S.B. vol. xxiv. 507; Records, Nos. 18–21 of autotype plate; A.A. p. 412, pl. xv. 20 (with the reverse upside down); and P.E. vol. ii. p. 96, pl. xxxvii. 18, 19.

The coin figured in A.A. pl. xv. 20, and as No. 18 of Records, and the coins Nos. 43, 44, of J.R.A.S. Vol. XII. o.s. Pl. II., have the bird as in the coins of Kumâra Gupta. The others have the degraded device which Thomas describes as "a small altar, which may be intended for the Mithraic altar of the gold coins, or for the conventional shrine of the sacred *Tulsî* of the Hindus." The same writer observes that this device "may be traced as the distinctive emblem of the Gurjjara successors of Skanda Gupta, and may be followed in its course on the copper-plate grants of Prasânta Râja, a monarch devoted to the worship of the sun" (J.R.A.S. Vol. I. N.S. p. 262). I have not been able to verify the allusions made by Mr. Thomas, but I prefer to follow Sir A. Cunningham in regarding the obscure device in question as a corruption of the winged peacock, while admitting that the so-called altar retains little or no resemblance to a bird of any sort.

The Winged Peacock coins of Skanda Gupta of all

SKANDA GUPTA—*continued.*

varieties are remarkable for their extremely rough execution. Few of them approach a circle in form, and many are little more than fragments. The letters of the legends, however, are in high relief, and easily legible, though formed in a very irregular and careless fashion. The weight of these coins is necessarily very uneven, and varies from 22·5 to 33 grains.

The occurrence of the title Vikramâditya in association with the name of Skanda Gupta is interesting, because that title was more specially appropriated by Chandra Gupta II. But there is no doubt whatever as to the reading of the word Vikramâditya on the ten coins in the British Museum. The specimen figured has the legend *Śrî Vikramâditya Skanda Gupta.* The *k* in the conjunct character *Sk* is formed by a loop like a *v* attached to the lower limb of the *S.*

Eight coins in the B.M. are labelled as having the title *Paramâditya,* but six of these (in tray No. 3) are ordinary *Kramâditya* coins, the word *parama* belonging to the epithet *parama bhâgavata.* The last two coins in tray No. 3 appear really to have the title *Paramâditya* (incomplete), as well as *parama bhâgavata.*

As already noted, the Kramâditya coins at end of tray No. 3 have the reverse device distinctly in the form of a bird, as on the coins of Kumâra Gupta.

One is noteworthy for expressing medial *m* twice by three dots (·.·), and another twice expresses the same character by a single dot (.). This last coin seems to bear the legend *Parama bhâgavata mahâkshatrapa* [? *Skanda*] *Gupta Kramâditya.* The word *mahâkshatrapa* appeared to me to be distinct. This title, which means 'Great Satrap,' has not yet been found on any other Gupta coin, but Kumâra Gupta perhaps used the title *kshatrapa,* or Satrap, on his Horseman to Left gold coins.

Prinsep's specimens are said to have come from Kachchh, Kâṭhiâwâṛ, and Guzerât. Newton observes that "The coins

SKANDA GUPTA—*continued.*

of the Guptas do not appear to have been found in any part of the (Bombay) Presidency except Guzerât and Kâṭhiâwâṛ" (J Bo.Br.R.A.S. vol. vii. p. 35); but Kachchh should be added. Out of 236 coins sent in by the Rao of Kachchh, 235 belonged to the so-called 'altar' type of Skanda Gupta, with the legend *Para .... Śrî Skanda Gupta Kramâditya* (*ibid.* vol. vi. p. lxxviii).

The title Kramâditya occurs on the heavy (*suvarṇa*) Archer type gold coins of Skanda, on the gold coins of Vîra Sena (?), and on certain gold coins of Kumâra, which are supposed to belong to Kumâra Gupta of the local Magadha dynasty.

Bull Type.

Obv. Head of king to r., as usual, executed rudely, as in the Winged Peacock coins. Sometimes traces of corrupt Greek legend before face. No date.

Rev. Recumbent bull to r.

Marginal legend परम भाग वतश्री स्कन्द गुप्त क्रमादित्य, *parama bhâgavata S'rî Skanda Gupta Kramâditya*, 'the most devout worshipper of the holy one, S'rî Skanda Gupta Kramâditya.'

References and Remarks.

B M. **Prinsep.** Two poor specimens. (Pl. IV. Fig. 5.)
B.M. One poor specimen.
A.C. (Arch. Rep. vol. ix. p. 25, pl. v. 12.)

The type is also described in J.R.A.S. Vol. XII. o.s. p. 66, Pl. II. 45, 46; A.A. pl. xv. p. 19; Records, fig. 19 of autotype plate; J.A.S.B. vol. xxiv. p. 506 (class *d*); and P.E. vol. ii. p. 98. The execution of these coins is as rude as that of the Winged Peacock coins, and the legends and weights are equally irregular. The weight varies from 21 to 30 grains.

The recumbent bull device is found on the seals of the kings of Valabhi, who succeeded the Guptas in Guzerat and Saurâshṭra, and also on the coins doubtfully assigned to

SKANDA GUPTA—*continued.*

Krishṇa Râja Rashṭrakûṭa of the Dakhin, who seems to have flourished at the end of the fourth century A.D.[1] It also appears on the coins of Brihaspati Nâga, and on one type of the coinage of Deva Nâga, who lived at about the same time, and seems to have belonged to the Nâga dynasty of Padmâvatî, the modern Narwâr in the Gwâlior State.[2] The Nâga coins seem to me to be a little later in date than the Gupta.

UNCERTAIN.

Chaitya Type.

I quote verbatim Sir. A. Cunningham's description of a coin in his cabinet, which he doubtfully assigns to Skanda Gupta. It does not agree either in reverse device or legend with the Gupta coins, and seems to me to belong to the Saurâshṭran Satrap series, but I have not minutely examined the coin itself, although I have seen it:

"*No.* 8.—*Obv.* King's head with moustaches, to right.

"*Rev.* Chaitya symbol. Legend in old Gupta characters very much crowded together: *Mahârâjâ Kumâraputra Parama Mahâditya Mahârâjâ Skanda Gupta* ?

"Mr. Newton has published a similar coin (J.Bo.Br.R.A.S. vol. vii. p. 12, and fig. 13), of which he remarks that the title of Mahârâja refers it to the Gupta series, while the addition of the father's name forms a connecting link with the coins of the Satraps of Surâshṭra. Mr. Newton reads the name of the king as Rudra or Nanda. I think, however, that it is intended for Skanda Gupta, the letters being so crowded together, that only portions of them could be delineated on the coin. I should like to have read Deva Gupta; but there is a tail to the second letter on both coins, which points to *nd* or *ndr*. Perhaps the name may be *Chandra Gupta III.*, which would be a natural appellation of Kumâra's eldest son, as it has

[1] Cunningham's Arch. Rep. vol. ix. p. 29, pl. v. 26, with reference to J.Bo. Br.R.A.S. vol. xii. p. 214.

[2] Coins of the Nine Nâgas, by Cunningham (J.A.S.B. vol. xxxiv. p. 122, with plate). Figures 5 and 6 of the plate represent the coins of Brihaspati Nâga, and 13 and 14 those of Deva Nâga. See also Arch. Rep. vol. ii. pp. 307-310, and vol. vi. p. 178.

SKANDA GUPTA—*continued.*

always been a Hindu custom to name one child after its grandfather, just as Kumâra's own father Chandra Gupta II. was named after *his* grandfather Chandra Gupta I."[1]

A name which can be read Rudra, Nanda, Skanda, or Chandra, may fairly be regarded as illegible. Mr. Fleet examined the coin (Ind. Ant. vol. xiv. p. 67), but could not make out the legend with any certainty. He marks nearly every letter as doubtful.

FANTAIL PEACOCK TYPE.

Obv. Head of king to r., apparently without moustaches. Date in front of face in ancient numerical symbols. No corrupt Greek legend.

Rev. Peacock facing front, with expanded wings and outspread tail, as in the similar coins of Kumâra Gupta.

Marginal legend, with vowel marks complete, in variety *a*

विजितावनिरवनिपति श्री स्कन्द गुप्तो देवो (or **देवं**) **जयति**,
vijitâvanir avanipati S'rî Skanda devo (or *devaṁ*) *jayati*, 'victorious is his majesty, the lord of the earth, S'rî Skanda Gupta, who has conquered the earth'; and in

Variety *β* **विजितावनिरवनिपतिर्जयति देव स्कन्द गुप्तोयं**, *vijitâvanir avanipatir jayati deva Skanda Guptoyaṁ*, 'victorious is his majesty, this same Skanda Gupta, lord of the earth, who has conquered the earth.'

References and Remarks.—Variety a.

B M. Date ? 16[–]. (Pl. IV. Fig. 4.)

A.C. Two specimens. (Ind. Ant. vol. xiv. p. 67.)

Variety β.

B. No. 785.

A.C. 12 specimens (Ind. Ant. vol. xiv. p. 67). Of these one with date 144 is shown in Pl. IV. Fig. 3, and this coin and another dated 145 are figured in Arch. Rep. vol. ix. pl. v. 9, 10.

The type is also described in J.R.A.S. Vol. XII. o.s. Pl. II. 52, 53; J.A.S.B. vol. xxiv. p. 512; P.E. vol. i. p. 335; and Records, Nos. 24, 25 of autotype plate.

[1] Cunningham, Arch. Rep. vol. ix. p. 24, pl. v. 8.

SKANDA GUPTA—*continued.*

The dates read are 144, 145, [1]48, 149 or 147, and ? 16[–].

Mr. Freeling had one specimen, and Colonel Stacy and Mr. Thomas each had four specimens of the type.

The coins are found in the same localities as the similar coins of Kumâra Gupta, but seem to be less abundant.

The highest weight noted by Thomas is 35 grains. Eight fair specimens showed an average weight of 31·7, and none, I think, will be found to exceed 36 grains.

Sir A. Cunningham was inclined to attribute one of his specimens to Dâmodara Gupta of the Later dynasty, but Mr. Fleet shows that the supposition is untenable (Ind. Ant. vol. xiv. p. 67).

BUDHA GUPTA.

Fantail Peacock Type.

Obv. Head of king to r., without moustaches.
Date in ancient numerical symbols, in front of face. No corrupt Greek legend.

Rev. Peacock standing to front, with expanded wings and outspread tail.
Marginal legend, with vowel marks complete, **विजितावनिरवनिपति श्री बुध गुप्तो देवो जयति**, *vijitâvanir avanipati S'ri Budha Gupto devo jayati*, 'victorious is his majesty, S'rî Budha Gupta, lord of the earth, who has conquered the earth.'

References and Remarks.

B. One specimen. Date 174.

A.C. One specimen. Date 174. (Arch. Rep. vol. ix. p. 25, pl. v. 13.)

Dr. Swiney. One specimen. Date 174. Wt. 32. (J.R.A.S. Vol. XII. o.s. Pl. II. 55.)

A C. One specimen. Date ? 18[–]. From Sârnâth. (Arch. Rep. vol. ix. pl. 25, *note* and verbal communication; Ind. Ant. vol. xiv. p. 67.)

Six specimens only of this type are known. Five, all dated in 174, were obtained at Benares in 1835 by Sir A. Cunningham, and the first three coins above enumerated

BUDHA GUPTA—*continued.*

belong to that batch. I do not know what became of the other two. The sixth specimen, which is now in Sir A. Cunningham's cabinet, was obtained at Sârnâth near Benares. Mr. Fleet reads the date on the Benares coins as 175, and it was wrongly read by Mr. Thomas as 155, but Sir A. Cunningham observes (*loc. cit.*) that "the value of the decimal is known from my Jayanâth inscription, which is recorded in words as well as figures."

The inscription of Budha Gupta dated 165 is at Eraṇ in Mâlwâ, and his territory lay between the Jumna and Narbadâ.[1] It is scarcely possible that Benares should have been subject to his authority, and the coins obtained there were probably brought by pilgrims. If carefully looked for, other specimens ought to be obtainable in Central India.

Supplement.

I have described in detail all the known silver coins which can be ascribed to the Early or Imperial Gupta Dynasty. Sir A. Cunningham has described coins of certain successors of the dynasty, with similar devices and legends (Arch. Rep. vol. ix. pp. 26–31, pl. v. pp. 16–28) ; and in order to render my account more complete, I shall give a brief notice of these coins.

BHÎMA SENA.

Fantail Peacock Type.

Obv. As in coins of Budha Gupta, but head to l. Date illegible.
Rev. As in Budha Gupta's coins, substituting the name of Bhîma Sena for that of Budha Gupta.

References and Remarks.

B.M. Procured by Mr. H. Rivett-Carnac at Ajodhya, and presented by him (Arch. Rep. vol. ix. pl. v. 16). Fig. 17 of same plate seems to be similar, but the coin is much worn.

Nothing is known concerning Bhîma Sena. The legend, as published by Sir A. Cunningham, was not quite correctly read.

[1] See Corpus Inscr. Ind. vol. iii. p. 88, No. 19.

TORAMÂṆA.[1]

FANTAIL PEACOCK TYPE.

Obv. Head of king to l. Date in front of face.
Rev. As in coins of Budha Gupta, substituting name of Toramâṇa for Budha Gupta.

References and Remarks.

B.M. Bush and Baring. (Arch. Rep. vol. ix. pl. v. 18, 19.)

These are the only two known specimens. I agree with Mr. Fleet in reading the date on both as 52. Sir A. Cunningham reads 53 on his No. 19, but the 3 seems to me to be a blurred 2.

There are three similar coins with head to l. in B.M., presented by Miss Baring, on two of which the date seems to be 54, but I could not decipher the king's name. It did not appear to be Toramâṇa. I attach no importance to the circumstance that the king's head is turned to l. The Gupta gold series proves that it was a matter of indifference which way the king's effigy was turned.

ÎS'ÂNA VARMÂ.

FANTAIL PEACOCK TYPE.

Obv. Head of king to l. Date in front of face.
Rev. As in coins of Budha Gupta, substituting Îśâna Varmâ for Budha Gupta.

References and Remarks.

A.C. Procured at Râmnagar, the ancient Ahichchhatra in Barelî District, N.W.P. (Arch. Rep. vol. ix. pl. v. 20).

C. Two specimens, procured at Ajodhya (Ibid. pl. v. 21, 22).

All these specimens are, according to Sir A. Cunningham, dated 55, of which the interpretation is doubtful. The name was at first wrongly read Śânti Varma (Arch. Rep. vol.

[1] For the Eraṇ inscription of the reign of Toramâṇa see Corpus Inscr. Ind. vol. iii. p. 158, No. 36. He is also mentioned in the Gwâlior inscription of his son Mihirakula (Ibid. p. 161, No. 37.)

ÎSÂNA VARMÂ—*continued.*

xvi. pp. 79, 81). Îśâna Varmâ was one of the Maukhari, or Mukhara, dynasty, who ruled in part of Magadha, and were the rivals of the later Gupta dynasty, which ruled in another part; and he was the contemporary and opponent of the Later Kumâra Gupta, who flourished about A.D. 550. See l. 5 of Aphsaṛ inscription of Âditya Sena in Corpus Inscr. Ind. vol. iii. p. 206.

Mr. Fleet examined two specimens, and observes that "on the obv. of the coin figured by General Cunningham as No. 22, in front of the king's face there are two marks, which may perhaps be the numerical symbols for 40, 60, or 70, and 5. But they are very imperfect and doubtful." "On the dated coins," he says, "the head and neck of the peacock are turned to the proper right, as in the early Gupta coins; in the coin without a date, they are turned to the proper left" (Ind. Ant. vol. xiv. p. 68).

COINS OF KINGS OF VALABHI.

TRIDENT TYPE.

Sir A. Cunningham gives a brief account of these coins in Arch. Rep. vol. ix. p. 28, pl. v. 23, 24, but they require more exhaustive examination than they have yet received. As I am not prepared to discuss them at length, I content myself with a mere reference to the published accounts. Prinsep notes that several hundred of coins of this class were found buried in the ruins of Puragaṛh, twenty miles west of Bhoj in Kachchh (J.A.S.B. vol. iv. p. 687). These coins were discussed by Mr. Thomas in J.A.S.B. vol. xxiv. p. 508; in his paper on the so-called Sâh kings in J.R.A.S. Vol. XII. (o.s.); and in P.E. vol. ii. p. 100.

The reverse device is similar to that of the unique Trident coin of Kumâra Gupta published by Mr. Newton.

The three Trident coins in the Bodleian probably belong to this class.

? KRISHṆA RÂJA RÂSHTRAKÛṬA.

Bull Type.

Obv. Rude head of king with moustaches to r.
No trace of either legend or date.

Rev. As in Bull type of Skanda Gupta. Legend in modified Gupta characters, read by Cunningham as *Parama Maheśwara, Mahâditya* (or *Mahâkshatra*) *pâdânudhyâta S'rî Krishṇa Râjâ.*

Coins from the Nâsik District, Bombay, supposed to belong to Krishṇa Râja Râshtrakûṭa, a king of the Dakhin, *circâ* A.D. 375–400 (Arch. Rep. vol. ix. p. 30, pl. v. 26). The legends require further examination. Mr. Fleet reads *parama mâheśwara-mâtâpitṛi-pâdânudhyâta Śrî Krishṇa râja*, and translates, 'The glorious Krishṇa Râja, who is a devout worshipper of (*the god*) Maheśvara, (*and*) who meditates on the feet of (*his*) parents' (Ind. Ant. vol. xiv. p. 68).

Chapter X.—Catalogue of Copper Coins.

Contents.

CHANDRA GUPTA II.

(I.) Umbrella Type.

Obv. King standing to l., 'kitcat' figure, the feet not being shown. An attendant (? female) holds over his head an umbrella with streamers or fillet attached. King bareheaded; with r. arm raised, the elbow being sharply bent, and the hand open and empty. No legend.

Rev. Garuḍa, with wings and human arms, facing front, standing on thick horizontal line, running across coin, in or near the centre. In exergue the legend महाराज श्री चन्द्र गुप्तः, *Mahârâja S'rî Chandra Guptaḥ.*

CHANDRA GUPTA II.—*continued.*

References and Remarks.

B. Elliott. No. 752. One of three coins of this type collected by Tregear. The word *Guptaḥ* forms a second line below *S'rî Chandra*, and the letters of the legend have a peculiar curve to l. One of the Tregear coins was figured in P.E. pl. xxx. 11.

W.T. Bought in the bazaar at Pânîpat in the Panjâb. Much worn, but the umbrella is distinct. Wt. 70·8. Diameter ·82. (Pl. IV. Fig. 8.)

A.C. No. 1. Human arms of Garuḍa distinct. Wt. 75·5. Diameter ·9. (Pl. IV. Fig. 9.)

A.C. No. 2. Much worn. Wt. 102. Diameter ·8.

(II.) Standing King Type.

Obv. 'Kitcat' figure of king, as in Umbrella type, but, owing to smaller size of this type, less of the legs is shown. No attendant or umbrella. In one coin the king's l. hand is seen to rest on a sword. No legend.

Rev. Device as in Umbrella type. The human arms of Garuḍa are not distinctly shown. Legend **श्री चन्द्र गुप्तः**, *S'rî Chandra Guptaḥ*, or **चन्द्र गुप्तः**, *Chandra Guptaḥ*.

References and Remarks.

B M. Two specimens. Wt. 37 and 47. (Pl. IV. Fig. 10.)

B.M. I.O. One specimen. Wt. 29.

B. Three specimens; viz. **No. 750** in Elliott collection, in fair condition. Legend *Chandra Guptaḥ*.

No. 753, ditto, in inferior condition. Legend *Srî Chandra Guptaḥ*.

Not numbered, in fair condition. Legend as on No. 753. Two of these coins are probably the Tregear coins figured in P.E. pl. xxx. 12.

A.C. No. 1. Wt. 53·5. Diameter ·68.

A.C. No. 2. Wt. 51·5. Diameter ·66.

A.C. No. 3. Wt. 49·0. Diameter ·67. King's l. hand rests on sword. *Srî* of legend wanting.

A.C. No. 4. Wt. 45·0. Diameter ·61.

A.C No. 5. Wt. 35·5. Diameter ·67.

A.C. No. 6. Wt. 26·0. Diameter ·57. Garuḍa stands on a pedestal formed of two horizontal lines.

CHANDRA GUPTA II.—*continued.*

A.C. No. 7. Wt. 22·0. Diameter ·61. Pedestal as in last. Figure of king rounded off at hips. No sword. (Plate IV. Fig. 11.)

A.C. No. 8. Wt. 13·5. Diameter ·50. Small, much worn.

A.S.B. One specimen.

H. One specimen, from Ajodhya.

It appears plain that the coins of this type comprise at least two different values. It is impossible that the specimens weighing 53·5 and 13·5 grains respectively should belong to the same denomination. But most of the extant specimens are in such bad condition, and the original weights are therefore so uncertain, that I do not know where to draw the line.

(III.) Vikramâditya Bust Type.

Obv. Bust of king to l., on horizontal line, distant about one-third of diameter, or less, from lower margin.

King's r. arm bent, as in Umbrella and Standing King types, but a lotus-flower is held between finger and thumb.

Legend in exergue **श्री विक्रमादित्य**, *S'rî Vikramâditya.*

Rev. Garuḍa to front, on pedestal. Legend below **चन्द्र गुप्तः**, *Chandra Guptaḥ.*

Diameter ·6 to ·7.

References and Remarks.

B.M. Stacy. Figured in P.E. pl xxx. 13. Wt. 44. (Pl. IV. Fig. 12.)

B.M. Hay. Wt. 40·5. In good condition, except obv. legend. A rayed crescent above king's head. (Pl. IV. Fig. 13.)

Swiney Collection. P E. pl. xxx. 14. Also figured in A.A. pl. xviii. 15.

The breasts are strongly marked in the Stacy coin, and this circumstance led Thomas (J.A.S.B. vol. xxiv. p. 514) to describe the obv. bust as that of a female. The obv. device seems to be derived from that of the gold coins of Ooerke (Huvishka).

The three specimens referred to are the only ones I know of, and I do not know what has become of the Swiney coin.

CHANDRA GUPTA II.—*continued.*

(IV.) Chandra Head Type.

Obv. Head of king to l., occupying whole field. No legend.

Rev. Bird with expanded wings (Garuḍa) facing front, standing on horizontal line. Human arms not distinctly shown. Legend चन्द्र गुप्तः, *Chandra Guptaḥ.* In at least two sizes.

References and Remarks.—(1) *Larger size.*

B.M. Prinsep. In poor condition. Wt. 27·0. Diameter ·62.

B.M. Eden. In poor condition. Wt. 20.

B.M. No. 3. In poor condition. Wt. 18·0.

B.M. No. 4. In poor condition. Wt. 18·0.

H. From Ajodhya. This specimen has lines below the wings of the Garuḍa, which may be intended for human arms.

B. No. 754. In bad condition.

A.C. No. 1. In fair condition. Wt. 28·0 Diam. ·55. (Pl. IV. Fig. 14.)

A.C. No. 2. In poorer condition. Wt. 25·5. Diam. ·57.

A.C. No. 3. In poorer condition. Wt. 21·5. Diam. ·54.

A.C. No. 4. In poorer condition. Wt. 20·5. Diam. ·52.

A.C. No. 5. Much worn. Wt. 18·0. Diam. ·47.

A.C. No. 6. Very much worn. Wt. 17·5. Diam. ·54.

A.C. No. 7. Worn, small. Wt. 16·5. Diam. ·43.

A.C. No. 8. Worn, small. Wt. 16·5. Diam. ·43.

(2) *Smaller size.*

B.M. Two specimens. Weight 9·5 and 11 respectively.

H. Three specimens from Ajodhya, one of which is now in author's possession.

B. Not numbered. In bad condition.

A.S.B. Many specimens; no details stated.

Lucknow Museum. Several specimens; no details stated.

A.C. No. 9. Worn. Wt. 13. Diam. ·42. (Pl. IV. 15.)

A.C. No. 10. In very bad condition. Wt. 12·5. Diam. ·53. In this coin the king seems helmeted.

A.C. No. 11. In very bad condition. Wt. 12·5. Diam. 40.

A.C. No. 12. In very bad condition. Wt. 12·5. Diam. 41.

A.C. No. 13. In very bad condition. Wt. 10·5.

A.C. No. 14. In very bad condition, very minute. Wt. 9·5.

A.C. No. 15. In very bad condition, very minute. Wt. 6·5.

A.C. No. 16. In very bad condition, very minute. Wt. 4·5, but doubtful, and may belong to Vase type.

CHANDRA GUPTA II.—*continued.*

It is obvious that all these coins, the weights of which range from 6·5 to 28 grains, cannot possibly be of one denomination, but the particulars above given show that the gradation in size and weight is so gradual that it is very difficult to draw a line anywhere. The coins are all in more or less bad preservation, and the weights consequently give very uncertain guidance. It is, however, certain that the extant specimens belong to at least two denominations. I am unable to come to any certain conclusion as to what these denominations were. The coins of this type are common, when compared with the other Gupta copper coins. I suspect that many exist in private collections, for such minute and ill-preserved coins are not readily recognized. I found one among the unclassed coins in the Bodleian cabinet.

KUMÂRA GUPTA.

Umbrella Type.

Obv. As in Umbrella type of Chandra Gupta II.

Rev. Ditto, but the initial letter of the king's name appears to be *K*, the rest of the name is lost.

References and Remarks.

The existence of this type of Kumâra Gupta's coinage is perhaps doubtful, and rests on a single very imperfect specimen in the possession of Sir A. Cunningham, who procured it at Ahichchhatra (Râmnagar) in the Barelî District, N.W.P. The last letter of the defaced legend is the first letter of the king's name, and certainly seems to be a *K*, and nothing else. I have examined it several times, and do not see how it possibly can be a damaged *Ch.* If the initial letter of the name was *K*, as it apparently is, the name must have been Kumâra. The syllables *râja S'rî* before the damaged name are quite plain.

The coin is in such bad preservation that I have not attempted to have it photographed.

KUMÂRA GUPTA.

Standing King Type.

Obv. Device as in Standing King type of Chandra Gupta II. The king wears a *dhotî*, or waistcloth, the folds of which are indicated. No legend.

Rev. Bird (Garuḍa) as in coins of Chandra Gupta II. Legend in exergue **श्री कुमार गुप्त**, *S'rî Kumâra Gupta.*

References and Remarks.

B. No. 751. Collected by Tregear, probably at Ajodhya. Unique. Note the modern form of *d.* An eye-copy of the legend is given in the annexed woodcut :

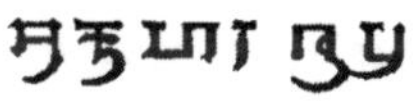

This is the only copper coin which we can affirm with certainty to have been struck as such by Kumâra Gupta. Sir A. Cunningham's specimen of his Umbrella type is doubtful. The copper coins of Kumâra Gupta and Skanda Gupta found in Kâṭhiâwâṛ, which resemble the silver coinage, and are noticed subsequently, may be ancient forgeries.

CHANDRA.

Vase Type.

Obv. The name **चन्द्र** *Chandra* inscribed horizontally across the field. In the smaller coins a crescent above the name.

Rev. A short-necked broad vase, with streamers proceeding from it, or vertical lines on each side. No legend. In two sizes.

(1) *Larger size.*

A.C. Wt. 13. (J.A.S.B. vol. xxxiv. p. 125, pl. xviii. 20.)

(2) *Smaller size.*

A.C. No. 1. A flower? above vase, and a vertical line on each side of vase, in lieu of streamers. Crescent above name. Wt. 7. Diameter ·42. In poor condition. (Plate IV. Fig. 16.)

A.C. No. 2. Similar, but in worse condition, and indistinct. Wt. 5·5.

A.C. No. 3. Very minute, in bad condition. Wt. 3·5. Diameter ·3. This coin and No. 2 seem to have streamers from mouth of vase. One is figured as figure 21 in J.A.S.B. *loc. supra cit.*

CHANDRA—*continued.*

The identity of the Chandra named on these coins is uncertain. He may be the Chandra, who recorded the inscription on the Iron Pillar at Delhi.[1] Sir A. Cunningham supposed him to be Chandra Gupta II., but the coins in question are quite different from those of the Guptas, and are related to the coins of the Nâga dynasty and of Paśupati of Nepâl (described in J.A.S.B. *loc. sup. cit.*). The Paśupati coins with similar vases are found in Nepâl.

The Chandra coins are in poor preservation, and I cannot determine their standard, but they certainly occur in two sizes. Some specimens of the smaller size are in the cabinet of the Asiatic Society of Bengal.

SUPPLEMENT.

UNCERTAIN.

Mr. Theobald has a small copper coin, weighing 25 grains, with the legend **-न्द्र** [or **द्र**] **महाराज श्री**, *-ndra* [or *-dra*] ***Mahârâja Śrî***, which may possibly belong to Chandra Gupta II., but the coin is in very bad preservation, and it is impossible to assign it.

A copper coin, with traces of gilding, in possession of Mr. H. Rivett-Carnac, appears to be an ancient forgery of the common variety of the Archer gold coins of Chandra Gupta II.

COPPER COINS OF KUMÂRA GUPTA AND SKANDA GUPTA, AGREEING IN DEVICE AND LEGEND WITH THE SILVER COINS.

The following notes record all that I can discover concerning the copper Gupta coins, which resemble the silver coinage. They may all be ancient forgeries, but, if they are, it is odd that such a considerable number of them should be found. The question of their genuineness deserves fuller examination than I have been able to give it. Some are certainly forgeries.

[1] Corpus Inscr. Ind. vol. iii. The name used to be read Bhâva or Dhâva.

Coins presented by the Thakur of Morvi, and exhibited at the meeting of the Bombay Branch of the Royal Asiatic Society on the 11th July, 1867, by the President, the Honourable Mr. Justice Newton.

"Four copper Gupta coins. Scarcely any portion of the legend is visible, but I recognize the coins as SKANDA GUPTA's" (p. xiv).

At the same meeting Mr. Newton also exhibited the following coins:

"Presented by the Chief of Walla.

Twenty copper coins of one of the Gupta kings, probably KUMÂRA, though scarcely a letter of the legend is left on any of them. The thin film of silver, with which some of them were originally covered, is still to be seen, and they thus add to the evidence which we already possess that the introduction of coinage did not long precede the idea of making it a means of fraud" (p. xv).

"The President also presented to the Society, on behalf of Captain Watson, Political Agent in Kâṭhiâwâṛ, fifteen small copper coins, on which he remarked that sufficient of the legend remained to enable him to identify them as the coinage of KUMÂRA GUPTA, the complete legend being *Parama Bhâgavata, Râjâdhirâjâ Kumâra Gupta Mahendrasya.*"

These coins, he added, were evidently a portion of the same hoard as those sent by the Chief of Wallâ, and Captain Watson stated that they formed part of a number dug up on the site of the ancient city of Valabhi.

Captain Watson's letter accompanying the coins was as under:

"I send you herewith some small copper coins found at Wallâ—a tolerably large hoard was dug up on the site of the ancient city of Valabhi. I have got eight besides those I send you, which I have given to two natives of Kâṭhiâwâṛ, to see if they can decipher any of the marks. I will send you the eight referred to shortly. Five of those I send are in pretty good preservation for copper coins. The rest have scarcely any marks left to decipher—a crescent or moon is very distinct on some of them. I trust during the rains to be able to procure more" (p. xviii).[1]

In the same volume Mr. Newton describes a copper coin

[1] Bo.Br.J.R.A.S. vol. ix. pp. xiv, xv, xviii.

of Swâmî Chashtana, father of Jaya Dâmâ, which belonged to Dr. Bhau Dâjî.[1] The coin resembles the earlier ones of the so-called Sâh kings. The obverse head is more finely executed than usual, and the legend, which ran all round the margin, as in some of the Bactrian hemidrachms, though illegible, caused Mr. Newton to "think that some at least of the Greek letters were correctly cut." The reverse devices consist of a wavy line with three-lobed *chaitya* emblem, a sun of sixteen rays, and two crescent moons.

"The weight of the coin is twenty-three grains, but several grains have been lost by chemical change and cleaning. The legend on the reverse is accurately copied in the figure, but I regret that I am unable to decipher it entirely. The whole, however, with the exception of the four letters enclosed below in brackets, may be read with certainty:

"*Râjno Mahâkshatrapasa* (*Syamo?*) *tika putrasa Chashtanasa* (*dala?*) *rumna*" (*sic*).

Cunningham points out (*ibid.* p. cix) that on the right half of the coin the ruler's name is repeated in Ario-Pâlî, as *Chashtanasa.* "The Indian and Aryan names are brought together."

Cunningham and Newton were certain as to the Arian name on a coin of Nahapana, but were not quite certain about the name of Chashtana in the Arian character.

I presume that this copper coin of Chashtana was the model of the copper coins of Kumâra and Skanda Gupta referred to above, if they are not merely forgeries of the silver coinage. Dr. Bhau Dâjî also possessed two copper coins of Jaya Dâmâ (*ibid.* p. xxv).

The British Museum has several specimens of minute copper coins resembling the silver in type. All are in bad condition. The only one at all decipherable has on obv. the usual head, rudely executed, and on rev. remains of a (?) trident, and distinct legend *Gupta Mahendrâd*[*itya*]. It must be assigned to KUMÂRA. The copper is good colour, and shows no sign of plating.

[1] *Ibid* p. 4, and fig. 4 of unnumbered plate, 'On Recent Additions to our Knowledge of the Ancient Dynasties of Western India.'

CONTENTS OF THE PLATES OF COINS.

PLATE.	FIGURE.	METAL.	REIGN.	TYPE AND VARIETY.	REFERENCE.
I.	1	AV	Chandra Gupta I.	King and Queen	B.M., purchased
,,	2	,,	Samudra Gupta	Tiger	,, Eden
,,	3	,,	(?) Samudra Gupta, Kâcha	Standard	,, Prinsep
,,	4	,,	Samudra Gupta	As'wamedha	,, Eden
,,	5	,,	,,	Lyrist, var. α	,, ,,
,,	6	,,	,,	,, ,, β	,, I.O.
,,	7	,,	,,	Javelin, var. 1	,, Prinsep
,,	8	,,	,,	,, ,, 1	,, Eden, *obv.* only
,,	9	,,	,,	,, ,, 3	,, Bush ,,
,,	10	,,	,,	Archer, ,, α	,, Eden
,,	11	,,	,,	Battle axe, var. α	,, Bush
,,	12	,,	,,	,, ,, β	,, Eden, *obv.* only
,,	13	,,	Chandra Gupta II.	Couch	,,
,,	14	,,	,,	Archer, Cl. I., var β	,, I.O.
,,	15	,,	,,	,, Cl. II., var. α	,, Eden
,,	16	,,	,,	,, ,, ,, β	,, I.O., *obv.* only
II.	1	,,	,,	,, ,, ,, δ	,, ,,
,,	2	,,	,,	,, heavy	,, Marsden, mlvi
,,	3	,,	,,	Horseman to r.	,, Prinsep, No 1
,,	4	,,	,,	Lion-Trampler, var. α	,, Swiney, No.5
,,	5	,,	,,	Combatant Lion	,, Swiney, No.4
,,	6	,,	,,	Retreating Lion	,,
,,	7	,,	,,	Umbrella, var. α	,, Eden, No. 1
,,	8	,,	,,	,, ,, β	,, ,, No. 2
,,	9	,,	Kumâra Gupta	Swordsman	,, Prinsep
,,	10	,,	,,	Archer, Cl I., var. α	,, Eden
,,	11	,,	,,	,, Cl. II.	,, I.O.
,,	12	,,	,,	,, heavy	,, P. Knight
,,	13	,,	,,	Horseman to r., var. γ	,, Bush
,,	14	,,	,,	,, l.	,, No. 1
III	1	,,	,,	Peacock, var. α	,, Lind
,,	2	,,	,,	,, ,, β	,, I.O.
,,	3	,,	,,	Combatant Lion	,, ,,
,,	4	,,	,,	Two Queens	,, R. Carnac
,,	5	,,	,,	As'wamedha	A.C.
,,	6	,,	Skanda Gupta	King and Queen	B.M., Prinsep
,,	7	,,	,,	Archer	,, I.O., No. 2
,,	8	,,	,,	Archer, Kramâditya	,, Prinsep
,,	9	,,	Prakâs'âditya	Lion and horseman	,, R.S.
,,	10	,,	,,	,,	,, I O. No. 1
,,	11	,,	Nara	Archer	,, Yeames
,,	12	,,	Kramâditya	Bull	,, R. Carnac
IV.	1	AR	Chandra Gupta II.	Vikramâditya	,, Bird
,,	2	,,	Kumâra Gupta	Winged peacock	,, Prinsep
,,	3	,,	Skanda Gupta	Fantail peacock, date, 144	A.C.
,,	4	,,	,,	,,	B.M.

CONTENTS OF THE PLATES OF COINS—*continued.*

PLATE.	FIGURE.	METAL.	REIGN.	TYPE AND VARIETY.	REFERENCE.
IV.	5	AR	Skanda Gupta	Bull	B.M.
,,	6	,,	,,	Vikramâditya	,,
,,	7	,,	,,	Kramâditya	,,
,,	8	Æ	Chandra Gupta II.	Umbrella	W.T.
,,	9	,,	,,	,,	A.C.
,,	10	,,	,,	Standing king	B.M.
,,	11	,,	,,	,,	A.C.
,,	12	,,	,,	Vikramâditya Bust	B.M.
,,	13	,,	,,	,,	,,
,,	14	,,	,,	Chandra Head	A.C.
,,	15	,,	,,	,,	,,
,,	16	,,	Chandra	Vase	,,

The following Comparative Tables of Weights and Measures are reprinted, by kind permission of the Trustees, from those appended to the several volumes of the Catalogue of Coins in the British Museum.

TABLE

FOR

Converting English Inches into Millimètres

AND THE

Measures of Mionnet's Scale.

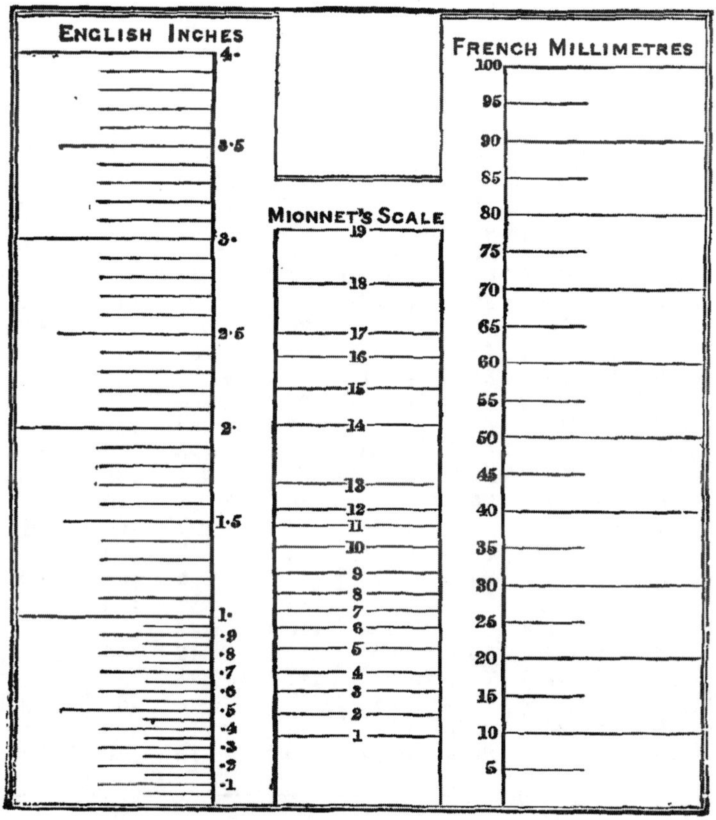

TABLE

OF THE

Relative Weights of English Grains and French Grammes.

Grains.	Grammes.	Grains.	Grammes	Grains.	Grammes.	Grains.	Grammes.
1	·064	41	2·656	81	5·248	121	7·840
2	·129	42	2·720	82	5·312	122	7·905
3	·194	43	2·785	83	5·378	123	7·970
4	·259	44	2·850	84	5·442	124	8·035
5	·324	45	2·915	85	5·508	125	8·100
6	·388	46	2·980	86	5·572	126	8·164
7	·453	47	3·045	87	5·637	127	8·229
8	·518	48	3·110	88	5·702	128	8·294
9	·583	49	3·175	89	5·767	129	8·359
10	·648	50	3·240	90	5·832	130	8·424
11	·712	51	3·304	91	5·896	131	8·488
12	·777	52	3·368	92	5·961	132	8·553
13	·842	53	3·434	93	6·026	133	8·618
14	·907	54	3·498	94	6·091	134	8·682
15	·972	55	3·564	95	6·156	135	8·747
16	1·036	56	3·628	96	6·220	136	8·812
17	1·101	57	3·693	97	6·285	137	8·877
18	1·166	58	3·758	98	6·350	138	8·942
19	1·231	59	3·823	99	6·415	139	9·007
20	1·296	60	3·888	100	6·480	140	9·072
21	1·360	61	3·952	101	6·544	141	9·136
22	1·425	62	4·017	102	6·609	142	9·200
23	1·490	63	4·082	103	6 674	143	9·265
24	1·555	64	4·146	104	6·739	144	9·330
25	1·620	65	4·211	105	6·804	145	9·395
26	1·684	66	4 276	106	6·868	146	9·460
27	1·749	67	4 341	107	6·933	147	9·525
28	1·814	68	4·406	108	6·998	148	9·590
29	1·879	69	4·471	109	7·063	149	9·655
30	1·944	70	4·536	110	7·128	150	9·720
31	2·008	71	4·600	111	7·192	151	9·784
32	2 073	72	4·665	112	7·257	152	9·848
33	2·138	73	4·729	113	7·322	153	9·914
34	2·202	74	4·794	114	7·387	154	9·978
35	2·267	75	4·859	115	7·452	155	10·044
36	2·332	76	4·924	116	7·516	156	10 108
37	2·397	77	4 989	117	7·581	157	10·173
38	2·462	78	5·054	118	7·646	158	10·238
39	2·527	79	5·119	119	7·711	159	10·303
40	2·592	80	5·184	120	7·776	160	10·368

TABLE

OF THE

Relative Weights of English Grains and French Grammes.

Grains.	Grammes.	Grains.	Grammes.	Grains.	Grammes.	Grains.	Grammes.
161	10·432	201	13·024	241	15·616	290	18·79
162	10·497	202	13·089	242	15·680	300	19 44
163	10·562	203	13·154	243	15·745	310	20·08
164	10·626	204	13·219	244	15·810	320	20·73
165	10·691	205	13·284	245	15·875	330	21·38
166	10·756	206	13·348	246	15·940	340	22·02
167	10 821	207	13·413	247	16·005	350	22·67
168	10·886	208	13·478	248	16·070	360	23·32
169	10·951	209	13·543	249	16·135	370	23·97
170	11·016	210	13·608	250	16·200	380	24·62
171	11·080	211	13·672	251	16·264	390	25·27
172	11·145	212	13·737	252	16·328	400	25 92
173	11·209	213	13·802	253	16·394	410	26·56
174	11·274	214	13·867	254	16·458	420	27·20
175	11·339	215	13 932	255	16·524	430	27·85
176	11·404	216	13·996	256	16·588	440	28·50
177	11·469	217	14·061	257	16·653	450	29·15
178	11·534	218	14·126	258	16·718	460	29·80
179	11·599	219	14·191	259	16·783	470	30·45
180	11·664	220	14·256	260	16·848	480	31·10
181	11·728	221	14·320	261	16·912	490	31·75
182	11·792	222	14·385	262	16·977	500	32·40
183	11·858	223	14·450	263	17·042	510	33·04
184	11·922	224	14·515	264	17·106	520	33·68
185	11·988	225	14·580	265	17·171	530	34·34
186	12·052	226	14·644	266	17·236	540	34·98
187	12 117	227	14·709	267	17·301	550	35·64
188	12·182	228	14·774	268	17·366	560	36·28
189	12 247	229	14·839	269	17·431	570	36·93
190	12·312	230	14·904	270	17·496	580	37·58
191	12·376	231	14·968	271	17·560	590	38·23
192	12·441	232	15·033	272	17·625	600	38·88
193	12·506	233	15 098	273	17·689	700	45·36
194	12·571	234	15·162	274	17·754	800	51·84
195	12·636	235	15·227	275	17·819	900	58·32
196	12·700	236	15·292	276	17·884	1000	64·80
197	12·765	237	15·357	277	17·949	2000	129·60
198	12·830	238	15·422	278	18·014	3000	194·40
199	12·895	239	15·487	279	18·079	4000	259·20
200	12·960	240	15·552	280	18·144	5000	324·00

INDEX.

CORRIGENDA ET ADDENDA.

PAGE LINE

10, 2, Saurâshṭra. The form Surâshṭra is also used. I have followed Mr. Fleet's authority.

16, 9, etc. The name of the queen of Chandra Gupta I. is written Kumâra, not Kumârî, in the inscriptions.

19, n.2. *For* Panjab *read* Panjâb.

20, 9. An alto-rilievo representing Herakles strangling the Nemean lion was discovered in 1882 by Sir A. Cunningham at Mathurâ. It is now in the Indian Museum, Calcutta, and is fully described in Dr. Anderson's admirable Catalogue of the Archæological Collections in that institution, Part I. page 191.

23, 31. I hope to show in another place that plastic art in India was considerably influenced by the school of Pergamon.

24, 25. The impress of the school of Scopas of Paros can be traced on early Buddhist sculpture.

26, 32. For *ambujâsinâ* read *ambujâsanâ*. The epithet occurs in Daśakumâracharitam, I. p. 27 (Bombay ed. 1883).

27, n. 2, *add*. Dr. E. W. West, in his Notes on Indo-Scythian Coin Legends (*ibid.* pp. 236–239), supports Dr. Stein's interpretation of the names of the deities on the coins, and shows that the second P in ΑΡΔΟΧΡΟ should probably be read as having the value of *sh*. A paper on the subject by Mr. Rapson is in the press.

29, 6. *For* Senapati *read* Senâpati.

29, 19. *For* Kodes *read* Hyrcodes (ΥΡΚΩΔΟΥ), and add reference to Gardner's Catalogue of Coins of Greek and Scythic Kings of Bactria and India, p. 117, plate xxiv. 8–13.

37, 22. Mr. Rapson has pointed out to me that the epithet *pratiratha*, like *pratihasta*, is used simply in the sense of 'opponent,' and that *apratiratha* should be translated as 'he who has no rival.' This correction is to be applied wherever the word *apratiratha* occurs.

56, n. 2, *add*. In Wilson's trans. of act ii. of the Mudrâ-Râkshasa the three names Kusumapura, Pushpapura, and Pâṭaliputra are used indifferently. (*Specimens of Theatre of the Hindus*, 3rd ed. ii. 178–179.)

81. Dr. Hoernlé informs me that he has seen a Class II. A. Archer coin (apparently one belonging to Mr. Rivett-Carnac), on which the reverse goddess, instead of having her legs crossed in the usual way, has the l. knee raised with her elbow resting on it. Mon. a variety of 8*a*.

89. Dr. Hoernlé informs me that a Combatant Lion coin of Chandra Gupta II. obtained by Mr. Rivett-Carnac either in Oudh or a neighbouring district, has on the l. obv. the legend [भ]ट्ट सिंहघ्नाभिज्ञ, [*bha*]*ṭṭa siṅhaghnâbhijña*, 'the valiant, who is clever in the slaying of lions.' The portion of the legend, about half, on the r. obv. is lost. Mon. 8*a*. I presume that the nasal in *siṅha*, which Dr. Hoernlé gives as *anuswâra*, is really the guttural *ṅ*, as in the case of other coins.
